the happiness habits

transformation

MICHELLE REEVES

Matthew James Publishing Ltd
Unit 46 Goyt Mill
Upper Hibbert Lane
Marple
SK6 7HX

www.matthewjamespublishing.com

Second Edition: Published 2023

ISBN: 978-1-913230-54-8

To Stewart, Amelia and Sebastian,
who remind me every day what gratitude was
made for.

*

In loving memory of Barbara Kari who taught me
that every day is a blessing

The song is ended but the melody lingers on.
- Irving Berlin

ABOUT THE AUTHOR

In 2008 Michelle Reeves left behind corporate life in the UK and moved to China for four years where her life fell apart. A traumatic birth and treatment for post-natal depression left her broken and searching for a way back to her former self. Over time and through the combination of 8 Happiness Habits she went from functioning to flourishing, including running her own life coaching practice for over six years.

Michelle lives in the East of England, UK, with her husband, two children, and two crazy rescue cats: Bella and Ziggy.

Find out more about Michelle at

michellereeveswrites.com

PREFACE TO THE SECOND EDITION

When the Happiness Habits Transformation was first published in 2019 I focussed on sharing my personal story, how I discovered and used the eight habits plus the fascinating research studies which underpinned each one.

For this second edition, I wanted to bring my story right up to date and share how these habits are continuing to support me as I navigate a new season of my life through menopause and beyond. I hope that the new insights in chapter twelve will be helpful if you're on a similar journey.

It was also important to me to include stories of people who have woven the habits into THEIR own routines, in their own way and how each habit has affected their lives.

I'm so grateful to everyone that has shared their personal journey within these pages and my hope is that, with this book you now have in your hands, you have the tools you need to create your own happiness habits transformation, whatever stage of life you're in.

CONTENTS

"When the well's dry, we know the worth of water."
Benjamin Franklin

CHAPTER ONE
WHAT HAPPENED TO US?

We had it down. We were organised. We sparkled. We rocked our lives and lived them on our terms with cheeky drinks after work and a nice browse around the shops when we fancied it.

We did coffee. And the gym. We read books.

(Ok, the gym was optional...)

We had hopes and dreams and plans and we rocked our visions for the future.

We were optimistic and basked in the light of our potential.

But then somewhere along the way we lost our sparkle under a pile of to-do lists, missed boats, almost-but-not-quites and the general busyness of life.

Our routine is based on what everyone else needs. Our work and family life fill our days up to the brim and we squeeze in what we can for ourselves in between... which isn't much.

And, if we're totally honest, in the dim hours when the truth seeps out between the cracks, we realise we might have lost ourselves a little bit along the way.

And it feels baaad.

I want to let you know right off the bat that I've thought ALL these things.

I was in that same place you are, recognising that something had to change, that I needed to take a time-out (without feeling guilty about it) to rediscover a happier, more authentic and truly successful me.

So how about this...

How about we spend a little time getting that sparkle back? How about we work together to create a simple routine with time to focus on YOU, releasing you from the habit of negativity, boosting your self-esteem and helping you dream and plan out your biggest, scariest and most exciting goals?

Think of it as laying a new foundation... paving the way for sparkle, success and happiness!

What this book isn't... and what it is.

There are shelves full of self-help books written by experts selling you the latest idea, must-have, or foolproof method for upscaling your life. Promises abound... but what they often fail to recognise is that there's another element that can totally screw up their systems... YOU.

When I searched around unsuccessfully for the 'magic' system that would work for ME I tried so many different things… positive psychology, affirmations, journaling, chanting, setting intentions, manifesting… and all of them had their benefits but I struggled to fit them into my busy life. I picked one up and tried it on for a while, but it was never really a good enough fit. So, after a while, it would start to lapse and ended up never really delivering what I was searching for.

Let me be clear from the start: I don't have a PHD, a research fellowship or a string of letters after my name. While I've had multiple professions, most recently I ran a life and mindset coaching business for over six years, and I'm fascinated by habit strategy - the way our physical and mental habits structure our lives. But probably just like you, I also have many other roles; wife, author, friend, sister and daughter, plus chauffeur-cook-wardrobe-assistant-mentor-ticklemonster-and-bean-bag for my two adorable kids. Let's be honest here; I wrestle most days into submission.

I know how difficult it can be to carve out the time for personal growth, so this book isn't a prescription that you need to follow to the letter. And it doesn't promise to light up your world just by reading it.

But, based on my experience and the experiences of the students in my Happiness Habits Transformation Course that preceded this book, if you consciously create some space in your day, add a sprinkle of the happiness habits that work for you and build them into a routine that YOU can stick to, you might just surprise yourself by becoming the most positive, powerful and productive version of yourself you've ever known.

Does that sound a little selfish to you? Yes, I can see you flinching, but look, this is so important and it speaks directly to the focus of the whole of this book - if we don't prioritise ourselves we end up trying to fill the many roles we play in our lives from an empty cup. We keep going back to dig deeper and deeper until there's nothing left for us. That might sound like 'service' or 'duty' but I disagree. I say it's uneconomic. When our cup is empty and we keep on trying to perform at our best we end up exhausted, depleted, resentful even. How is that serving those around us? I'd argue that it doesn't serve anyone, let alone ourselves.

If instead we make a conscious decision to fill up our own cup first, building our energy, replenishing our health, positivity, confidence, inspiration and satisfaction regularly, that full cup will overspill into the rest of our lives, without leaving us completely drained.

And I think that's worth a little time and effort, don't you?

A note about active learning

As you read through this book you'll notice that there are spaces for you to make notes. While it might make you feel a bit rebellious to write in a book when we're often specifically told as children not to, I'm conscious that most of us (me included) tend to consume books passively, nodding along to the bits that interest us, frowning or 'humf'-ing at those that don't, before putting them down and moving on to the next. But real change comes from active engagement. And by that I mean not only reading the ideas here but reflecting on them, thinking about how they might apply to your life and what actions you could take to make them live for *you*. So I hope that you'll either use these spaces for your own notes, or, if you prefer, use sticky notes or a journal to capture your thoughts.

"Our strength lies in our weakness."
Ralph Waldo Emerson

CHAPTER TWO
THE LONG & WINDING PATH TO HAPPINESS

Before we set off on our journey together you might be wondering how I came to create The Happiness Habits Transformation. You see, I had a very personal reason for writing this book. A reason that takes me back to 2009 and the day that my daughter was born.

Over time I blocked out a large part of my daughter's early life, protecting myself. But here I'm going to go back to those early dark days and piece together what I can. Not for closure or resolution but because it was an important part of my journey and hopefully it will explain why the Happiness Habits Transformation has become such a powerful force in MY life and why I hope it will be in yours too. I also hope that it helps remove the stigma around mental health issues and that it helps you if you're feeling as lost and hopeless as I did.

So let's start at the beginning, shall we?

On June 25th 2009 Michael Jackson died.

I remember precisely where I was when I heard the news on CNN because I was lying in a hospital bed in Shanghai, just across the street from our apartment, willing our baby to grow.

She was the baby we thought we might never have. Back home in the UK I'd been diagnosed with unexplained infertility and told I'd have to start IVF treatment to get pregnant. Just as we were looking into what that would mean for us, Stewart, my husband, came home from work and asked how I felt about moving to China for a couple of years for the next stage in his career. I knew it was an experience of a lifetime so, even though I was doing really well in my own job in marketing in London, I resigned and we packed up our lives, heading out to Shanghai just months later.

To give you some context for what's to come, we were a couple that loved travel and adventure. We skied and scuba dived, drove around Europe and rode our motorbikes. We'd scoot off to Bruge or Barcelona for a weekend away at the drop of a hat, me on my much loved red, white and blue Honda RVF400 race-styled import, him on a bright red VFR750. So it wasn't just our house that we left behind, it was our way of life. But it was an exciting opportunity and we grabbed it with both hands.

We started fertility treatment in China in 2008 and after three failed attempts I fell pregnant later that year. For anyone who hasn't been through IUI (a type of fertility treatment similar to IVF) this was a blessing in more ways than one - having my husband stick a needle in my butt every night was not the most romantic experience!

When I received that call in November from the clinic to say that we were finally going to become parents I ran straight to Mothercare on Haui Hai Lu with my friend Amy and bought a soft toy rabbit and a baby gro. (We still have Bunny Boo Babs today, a bit raggerty, but much loved.)

My pregnancy was pretty normal at the beginning. But our baby girl had always been small for her dates and our week 34 scan showed that her slow growth had slowed too much and somehow my amniotic fluid level had started to drop. Ten days later she'd gained no weight at all and the fluid had dropped again, this time down to just under 7cm (values between 8-25 are considered to be normal[1]).

Our wonderful Chinese American obstetrician, Michelle, admitted me immediately so that we could be monitored closely. I was put on an IV drip, paddles were strapped to my belly and I watched as a graph of our baby's heartbeat spewed out on long sheets of paper, the nurses chatting in Mandarin around me. My husband and I were learning the language so I caught a word every so often. At first I tried to figure out what they were saying, but it was too exhausting, so in the end I let it wash over me. I remember thinking I should be so grateful to be sitting in a comfortable private hospital room, but just being too worried to appreciate it. Michelle popped in later and confirmed that so far everything was ok but I'd have to stay in overnight.

I didn't go home until our baby was born two weeks later.

The following morning, my new daily feeding routine began. As well as breakfast, lunch and dinner the nurses brought me protein shakes three times a day, the kind a weight-lifter drinks. I breathed in thirty minutes of oxygen every few hours, which burned my nose and dried out my throat. I was given three steroid injections to help strengthen our baby's little lungs, preparing for the possibility of an early birth. (My obstetrician, Michelle, wanted to try and hold on until 37 weeks because there was no neo-natal ward at the expat hospital we were in.)

At a time when I should have been nesting at home it was all very scary and bright and real.

So I plugged in my laptop and listened to BBC Radio 2 over the internet, the reassuringly familiar voices of Alex Lester, Sarah Kennedy and Terry Wogan telling me the time at home, the weather, the news, anything to still my frantic mind. At this point Stewart had joined me in the hospital, working from a desk in the corner of my room and going back to our apartment to sleep at night.

And all the time I had to eat, eat, eat in the hope that it would help our tiny baby girl to grow.

But while my weight ballooned. Our baby girl's didn't budge an ounce.

This meant it was possible my placenta wasn't functioning properly and was starting to harden and calcify (before 37 weeks this can mean baby doesn't get enough oxygen or other nutrients). At the same time the level of amniotic fluid was dropping, leaving our daughter in a dangerous position. Guilt and anger at my own body flooded through me – why had it stopped nourishing and protecting our baby?

Then the fear began to creep through my veins. After everything we'd been through to get this far, months of fertility treatment with day after day of drugs and injections I started to believe that I wasn't actually meant to be a Mother.

The days passed slowly and I had a scan every morning to check baby's weight and size. I craved seeing her bobbing about on the screen, reassured by knowing that she was still there, still alive, still moving. I began to obsess about fluid levels and heart rates, learning more than I ever wanted to know about the importance of every little ounce and bpm.

Little did I know that obsession was a precursor of things to come.

On the morning of 6 July 2009, I had my daily scan as usual, Stewart joining me so we could see our baby together. But this morning something was different. We could never understand what the technicians were saying to each other but usually our obstetrician translated for us. This time she was silent, watching the monitor intently. A few slow minutes later she told us that our little baby girl's breathing had started to slow, slightly but significantly, and so she wanted to take her out now.

I would be having a C-section, at 36 weeks, in three hours time.

***

The birth wasn't exactly as we'd planned it...

I remember that my initial reaction wasn't fear, strangely, but excitement. I didn't think too much about the process, the epidural or the operation at that moment. I didn't even think about what having a premature baby would mean. After so long waiting at the hospital I just couldn't wait to meet our little girl!

Nurses came to prepare me for the operation and at 1.50pm I was helped onto a gurney. Stewart held my hand and kissed me goodbye – waiting behind while I was wheeled through a maze of corridors by an orderly.

We went up to the fourth floor of the hospital in a noisy goods lift alongside an elderly Chinese man in a wheelchair, just inches from my almost bare body. We glanced at each other and I wondered what he was thinking. Finally I was wheeled into a large white room and transferred to another table for my epidural. Our obstetrician, Michelle, was already there waiting for me, all prepared in her operating gown. The technician barked in Mandarin that I needed to lie on my side and stay completely still. The table was ice cold and uncomfortable and I felt like a beached whale. Michelle told me I would feel a little sting from the injection to numb the area before they performed the epidural.

Thinking back, I can't isolate the two things in my mind – all I can remember is the pain as the needle went in. And came out. And went in again. I kept thinking that this didn't seem right. I don't know how many times they tried to do the epidural, but I do remember Michelle holding my hand so tightly and telling me to try and stay calm. I know now that it took 45 minutes, and it wasn't entirely successful...

Eventually, they laid me on my back and I started to feel my legs go numb. I was wheeled into another room, the operating theatre, where thankfully Stewart was waiting for me. By this point I was scared. Michelle was barking orders and people were moving around the room with a sense of urgency. A curtain appeared across my chest between us and the medical team, cutting us off from what was about to happen. Stewart held my hand. I looked into his face with tears in my eyes.

I didn't feel the incision. But we both heard the rush of water as it escaped out of me and splashed on the floor.

Then I started to feel again.

Hands inside me, pulling, tugging. The pain started as a dull ache but grew quickly. Tears started running down my face and Stewart told the nurses that I could feel again, that I was in pain. But Michelle said it was too late, she had to take our baby now.

I couldn't believe this was happening. Was she ok? Was everything alright? I didn't care about anything else as long as our baby was safe, but the pain kept coming in waves.

And so my amazing husband did what he does best in stressful situations. He took charge.

Using a visualisation technique that we'd learned in preparation for the natural birth we'd hoped for, he took me to our favourite ski mountain at Mont Tremblant in Quebec. He made me feel the cold air on my skin, showed me the beautiful blue sky. He led me down the mountain as he had done countless times for real and I focussed every ounce of my being on that ski run.

What I couldn't see, what Stewart could see as he lifted his head to tell Michelle what I was feeling, was our doctor kneeling on the operating table, her hands in my belly up to her elbows, wrenching our baby out of my body. And knowing that now, I'm all the more grateful for his cool head.

And then suddenly she was out. Our beautiful little baby girl, just over 4lb in weight, joined us in the world. Not the smallest of babies, I know, but small enough. Through the blur of tears I wanted to see her, to hold her but the nurses put her in an incubator before I had the chance.

We agreed that Stewart should go to be with her. He released my hand… then… nothing.

I woke up out of a morphine-induced sleep back in our room. I had desperately wanted to do skin-to-skin and breastfeed from the start - along with everything else in my birth plan and ideal motherhood dream - but as I looked over I could see Michelle sitting on the sofa feeding our baby girl her first milk from a bottle, showing Daddy what to do.

She was so tiny, so fragile, it broke my heart.

Despite our traumatic birth experience, the nurses and doctors in China were amazing and without their help we wouldn't have had our miracle. It wasn't the fairytale birth that I'd planned for or hoped for, but after five years we finally had our baby girl - and we named her Amelia.

Nothing really prepares you for your first few days as a new Mum... and mine were as traumatic as the birth itself. Thankfully, my Mother flew out from the UK to help me, (I don't know what I would have done without her calm confidence) and I did what I could those first few days, but Amelia struggled to feed well and, without the support of a health visitor or midwife visiting me at home we had no idea that she wasn't gaining the right amount of weight. When I took her back to the hospital for a check-up they said she hadn't put on any weight in a week and was 'boney and emaciated'. I was barked at for not feeding her properly - I was doing the best I could but it clearly wasn't enough.

When the paediatrician left the room I sobbed hysterically in my own Mother's arms. My Mother is an incredible woman who's overcome her fair share of challenges, and while she held me tightly she knew that I needed to pull myself together for her granddaughter's sake. Her firm, guiding words shook me out of myself and into practical mode. We needed to move forward.

I was given a strict regime of breastfeeding every two hours round the clock and pumping extra milk after every feed. Feed, pump, rest briefly, feed, pump, rest briefly. It was a relentless schedule and pretty soon I was mentally and physically exhausted.

On top of this, our daughter did not sleep at night. She cried and cried as we walked her up and down our Shanghai apartment for hours at a time, thinking she had colic. We emptied bottles of Infacol, syringing it into her little mouth, hoping it would help. I realise now that she was probably just hungry, unable to take in enough of the goodness her tiny body needed because she was just too small.

Thankfully the strict regime worked though and she gradually started to gain weight. I dozed between feeds either on a chair or the cushioned window seat in the nursery, so that Stewart could get the sleep he needed to go to work. I almost forgot what it felt like to sleep in a bed. Slowly time passed but after a few weeks my Mother had to go back to the UK. The lack of sleep and support and constant stress of Amelia's weight gain left me ragged and withdrawn.

Then the obsession began...

I started obsessing about my milk and wrote down the length of each feed, timing them to the minute and keeping a detailed log. My journal entries from those first few weeks are full of anxiety, confusion and frustration.

"Now what do I do? When do I wake her? Breast or Bottle? When do I sleep? Express? Surely as she gets bigger she needs more milk than less? How do I know when she's hungry? How do I get her to feed? How do I know when to get her to take more and when to let her sleep?"

On our 6th wedding anniversary all I managed to write was "all morning feeds very sleepy, light sucking, no big gulps but swallowing every 2-3 sucks. Hope she's getting enough milk."

The stress and lack of sleep started to take its toll on my mind. From the elation of finally seeing our beautiful little girl in my arms after waiting and trying for SO long, I strangely began to feel no emotion towards her at all. I knew that I should be happy but I felt numb and ungrateful. With only 2-3 hours rest a night I was so tired, but I couldn't sleep. It was a struggle to even smile.

I started to separate myself from our expat friends, pulling out of meet-ups because I was embarrassed about how useless I was and felt guilty seeing how happy they were when I felt so empty.

And then thoughts started to pass through my head that I can't even bear to put into words here, strange, dark thoughts that rose up from I don't know where and scared me. I completely lost my confidence and in the grip of anxiety, I holed up in my 'baby bunker', struggling to leave the apartment for even the simplest of trips to the supermarket. I was in the grip of the most traumatic time in my life and I felt like I was losing my mind, but at the same time I was strangely detached from myself and everything around me.

Once a confident, successful career woman, I'd become a shell of my former self, operating on autopilot and barely smiling.

Finally it was Stewart who came back from a business trip and realised how badly I needed help. "Where's the happy, positive, fun-loving girl I met and married?" He asked.

I think I just shrugged.

"What hurts you, blesses you. Darkness is your candle."
Jalaluddin Mevlana Rumi

CHAPTER THREE
DISCOVERING THE HABITS

Eight months after our daughter was born I met with a clinical psychologist. In a distraught and tearful consultation I spoke, for the first time, about what I'd been going through, my feelings and the thoughts in my head. As the words and the tears flowed I felt a lightness come over me, like I'd been carrying a huge bag around and I was finally handing it over to someone else. At the end of our session she diagnosed me with Postnatal Depression.

My diagnosis wasn't the total relief it perhaps should have been. I saw the diagnosis as failure. Failure at what? At coping I think, at not living up to my own expectations of what kind of mother I was going to be. But she did tell me that the awful thoughts I was having were normal after the trauma I'd been through. She offered me anti-depressants but I didn't want to add to the cocktail of drugs I'd been taking for months so we turned to Cognitive Behavioural Therapy and she taught me coping strategies that I could use when the 'black days' came.

Slowly, over the course of our sessions the therapy brought me back from non-functioning to functioning again. As I worked through my emotions and stopped obsessing, I started to go out more, began a daily yoga practice, swimming, running and meditation, and cared about how I looked for the first time in months.

But brilliant as all this was, and it was utterly brilliant, the therapy wasn't enough.

Yes, working with my therapist got me from non-functioning to functioning (and I'll always be grateful for the intervention and the valuable lessons I learned). But as time went on I knew I needed to go one step further. So I read and read and read, devouring personal development books and blogs. It was that focus on my own personal development that took me beyond functioning to really rediscovering ME again, and ultimately kick-started my journey from functioning to fabulous. It opened up my mind again to growth and change, to releasing negative thoughts and letting go of the rules and expectations that governed my mindset.

RULES & EXPECTATIONS LIKE:

- ▶ When you're a new Mother you have to devote 100% of your time to your baby
- ▶ Mothers automatically know what their babies need and how to look after them

- Being a Mother is always the happiest time of your life
- I don't need to 'like' myself - there's more important things to do
- I can't have a baby AND personal goals AND a business
- I don't matter as much as my baby
- I won't be able to lose my baby weight for at least a year
- It's selfish to expect to spend time on myself
- You have to exercise for at least an hour or it doesn't do any good
- Everyone else is smiling so they must be happy with their lives

Over time I shaped and moulded everything I learned into a set of habits that both grounded me in the here and now and helped me see the beauty of future possibilities. And eventually I cemented those habits, the habits that drove me away from the ingrained negativity I'd come to live with, into a routine.

I called it my Happiness Habits routine.

And I started to dream again. Big, sparkly, exciting dreams that I couldn't even bear to mention to anyone else in case they never came true. Dreams about being happy and healthy and not running away from my thoughts. Dreams about purpose and passion and inspiring others. Dreams that eventually became goals and plans and led me to start my own coaching practice, where I helped amazing men and women to manage their mindset, leave behind their self-doubt and limiting beliefs and become the version of themselves they long to be. And, ultimately, writing this book for you.

I know how easy it is to lose yourself in the busy-ness of life. I struggled with my depression and am not ashamed to admit it took therapy, time and deep personal work to find my way back to me.

I know how it feels to be exhausted, lost, fed up of putting a brave face on things and guiltily wanting to find YOU again. I know what it's like to seem like you have it all on the outside, but feel something's missing on the inside. I know how it feels to shelve your dreams. To crave purpose and meaning for you because you know inside that if you're a happier you that joy will ripple out and touch your family, your friends, your business and the rest of your life.

I leaned in and focused every ounce of strength I had on my personal growth, on becoming aware of the stories I was telling myself, the negative self-beliefs that held me back.

And that is why I wanted to write this book, to share the tools and techniques I've learned to create a simple, daily routine that prioritises guilt-free space in our day for *us* and puts the focus back on *our* happiness.

Because I passionately believe that we all deserve the gift of inspiring, nourishing space in the day for us in order to show up in the rest of our lives as our most positive, powerful and productive selves.

We need this to create our lives instead of letting them happen around us, to decide how we want to feel each and every day and to make that happen through our thoughts, words and actions.

And the biggest transformations start with our daily habits.

HOW TO USE THIS BOOK

I'm going to share with you the eight habits that I use every day to inspire and motivate me to become the very best version of myself, in my personal and professional life.

We'll look at each habit in turn, with examples and exercises to help you to build the habit into your day. In my online course my students carved out 30 minutes each day to create their new Happiness Habits Transformation, but don't feel that you have to group all your new habits together in that way. As I said earlier this book isn't meant to be prescriptive, and I have no doubt that you'll take from it what works for you and leave the rest.

To help support the creation of your transformation, in chapter eleven we'll dive deeper into habit formation, and how to make your habits 'stick'. So for now, just think about how each habit could sit comfortably into your daily life and feel your way into it rather than trying to shoehorn them in one by one.

Are you ready? Ok, let's begin...

"The greatest weapon against stress is our ability to choose one thought over another."
William James

CHAPTER FOUR

MY FIRST HAPPINESS HABIT
*Awareness & why your thoughts
matter more than you think*

How aware are you of your thoughts?

What are you thinking as you start reading this chapter? Perhaps you're wondering where I'm going with this... perhaps you're thinking about something you've got planned for later on today... perhaps you're deciding to pause and grab a cup of coffee and a snack because you can't concentrate unless you plug that hungry-hole...

The thing is most of the time we're not really even aware of our thoughts. We think of them as just... well... us.

But learning to become more aware of our thoughts and how to actively manage them is a game changer when it comes to our daily happiness.

In the worst days of my depression, the 'black days', my mind was my inner enemy and its weapon of choice was negative thoughts. Those thoughts would circle round and round in my head, a personal propaganda campaign targeting my confidence and self-esteem. And the worst thing was that I believed them. I believed every negative and self-bashing 'story' my mind told me as the truth.

And this had a major impact on the 'results' I saw in my life. But how could something as simple as a thought have so much power?

What I've learned is that our thoughts have a major impact on our emotions, they literally create our feelings. And those feelings lead directly to our behaviours and ultimately to our results in life.

Consider this… if you're afraid of spiders and I asked you to visualise a big hairy tarantula just millimetres from your fingers, you'd probably start to FEEL something in your hand… a prickly, creepy, skin-crawling sensation… and you might move it. Even if there isn't a spider anywhere near you.

This is because our mind often doesn't see the difference between a strongly held belief and reality. And our beliefs start with our thoughts.

While I was sitting here writing this book, struggling with a line I was working on, a thought popped into my head; "Why can't I think of the right phrase here?" That thought was closely followed by "What if I get writer's block and can't finish the book?"; "What if I do finish it and my publisher hates it… what if no one reads it?!" Those thoughts spiralled around my head for a while, with my heart rate rising and my mind getting foggy and thick with worry. Pretty soon I was panicking when all that really happened was I couldn't find the words I was looking for!

Has that ever happened to you?

Thought loops and spirals like these can be so challenging. And they can be triggered by the simplest things, sinking us into an anxiety that we don't really understand and can't seem to shake. In the same way that we get into a habit of biting our nails or twirling a curl around a finger, thought loops can arise at particular times for us - when we're thinking about trying something new or challenging or stressful.

Stress literally changes how our brain functions, increasing the activity in the fear centre (called the amygdala) and decreasing activity in our rationalisation centre (the prefrontal cortex) which results in making those negative thoughts even more likely.[2]

Thought loops can be cyclical, following a circle of thoughts that ends up back at the same starting point, or spiralling so we start with one negative thought and somehow it descends into everything that's wrong with us and the world around us!

To add to that we have a built-in confirmation bias which means that when we have a negative thought that we believe strongly to be true, our mind naturally, but rather unhelpfully in this case, searches for evidence to prove us right, and ignores or rejects evidence that proves us wrong.[3]

So here I am sitting at my desk, thinking negative thoughts about my book. And guess what, I start to feel lousy. It begins as generalised worry, peaks as anxiety and plummets into hopelessness. If I don't get a handle on these feelings they could lead directly to a behaviour and result I'm going to regret later on - quitting writing this book altogether!

This pattern of thought, feeling, behaviour and results is so pervasive in our lives that we scarcely notice it happening. But it all starts with a single thought.

And that's why thought awareness - or mindfulness as it's commonly called - was my first transformational Happiness Habit. It's the foundation habit that underpins all the others.

By practising becoming aware of my thoughts for just 5-10 minutes a day I learned to live more in the NOW, rather than the future or the past (where so many of us hang out without even noticing it) and I realised that I actually get to choose how I want to feel and act rather than reacting to my thoughts or to life as it happens around me.

I call it living life with purpose, on purpose.

But I have to warn you... this is the habit that you're most likely to skip out of. Why? Because for most of us without the luxury of sitting on a beach sipping cocktails more than once in a blue moon, our lives are crazy busy. We're always on the go, from morning to night, adding to our never-ending to-do lists, commuting, working on our side-hustle, running errands, holding our home, family, business together, bouncing from one role to another as life demands it.

Even if we get to stop for a moment, without falling asleep or devouring Netflix, and try to sit still in our stream of thoughts, we can find ourselves racked with guilt for being unproductive. I have to admit that at the beginning I would sometimes skip days or whole weeks of my thought awareness practice for exactly these reasons.

And I'm gonna be totally honest with you here, becoming aware of the crazy, tumbling thoughts that whirl around our minds while all this is going on can feel difficult at best, at worst, totally exhausting.

As you've read earlier, when our daughter was born prematurely in 2009 I immediately began a round-the-clock feeding routine that meant all of my energy and focus was on her needs. Anything I needed got lost in the madness for a long time. I was shattered and scattered, my mind caught up in negative thought loops and anxiety that circled around and around in my head.

I worried about what was going to happen tomorrow or the next day... I obsessed about what happened the day or week before... I was lost in my mind, living life through my crazy thoughts.

And even after my therapy sessions had ended, there were days when I was deeply unhappy at a time when I could have been full of joy. I had no idea that it was my own self-limiting thoughts that were creating my unhappiness. I had no idea that I had a choice about how I felt.

When I first started to sit quietly and learn to 'listen' to my thoughts, I won't lie to you, it was scary. I felt like a crazy woman! Like I had no control over what my mind was doing, no way to stop the tumbling whirlwind of memories, ideas and projections.

But by being patient with myself and practising some simple exercises, I've learned to love my thought awareness practise, because it gifts me time to focus wholly and entirely on right now and reminds me every single day that my thoughts are just that, thoughts, and I don't have to let them control me or define me.

This short time by myself became a lifeline in my darkest days and I began to see flashes of the calm energy I so desperately longed for.

And I soon realised that the result was I reacted less and made more conscious decisions about the situations I found myself in, whether over time that was a toddler meltdown in the supermarket or a challenging situation in my business.

The benefits of learning to sit with my thoughts definitely outweighed the challenges.

As I moved into intentionally creating my Happiness Habits routine, I knew I wanted thought awareness to be one of the very first things I did, every day. I wanted to use it to start my morning with focus, setting a foundation for the rest of my day.

Even now, years later, when I wake up my head is often still so full of what happened yesterday that I wish I'd tackled differently, plans for the future and a long list of things I need to get done. But just 10 minutes or so practising being aware of my thoughts with curiosity and kindness helps me to release those thoughts so that I can concentrate on the important few rather than the trivial many.

Seriously, it's like an enema for my mind.

I'm more emotionally balanced, with a better sense of perspective that boosts my resilience when the you-know-what hits the you-know-what (and it's too early for cocktails!). And most importantly it reminds me that I always have a choice about how I respond to my thoughts.

I was first introduced to thought awareness as a short meditation practice at the end of my yoga classes in China. Meditation is a great way to experience thought awareness because it gives you a space to practice in, a 'home' if you like.

There are other ways to practise too, like journaling, walking or eating mindfully for example. But meditation is my personal favourite and so we're going to spend some time getting to know that 'home' a little better.

If you've ever tried meditation before and found it frustrating or uncomfortable you are not alone - I struggled SO hard with my early practises. But please don't let that make you skip the rest of this chapter! As I've learned over time and with experience and the right guidance, becoming aware of your thoughts can be as easy as sitting on a chair and breathing - and the benefits really can be remarkable.

Meditative techniques have been used for thousands of years and celebrities from Oprah Winfrey and Arianna Huffington to the late Kobe Bryant have talked about its positive impact on their lives.

And while I'm not going to promise that it's foolproof or instantaneous, studies have shown scientific evidence of positive changes in the brain that occur during meditation. A summary of this research by Dr. David Cox, Dr. Amishi Jha and Andy Puddicombe, co-founder of the Headspace meditation project points to over 160 studies that have found mindfulness practice having a positive and substantial effect on wellbeing. Research has even shown that meditation can cause parts of the brain associated with learning and memory to grow in size and those connected with stress and anxiety to shrink. From depression to immune function, creativity, sleep and mental health, meditation can have a transformative effect.[4]

Ultimately, in my experience, thought awareness is a great way to focus your mind on the here and now, at any time of day. To give this a try for yourself, or to restart a practice you've struggled with in the past, start by taking 5-10 minutes out of your day to sit quietly and simply watch your thoughts. Over time you can experiment with practising at different times of day and seeing what works best for you.

But first, let's dispel some myths about meditation...

MYTH #1
MEDIATION MEANS SITTING COMPLETELY STILL FOR HOURS AT A TIME.

Before I started my own mediation practice I envisaged having to sit in stillness for ages, willing myself not to scratch my nose or fidget, as serenity slowly descended upon me. This couldn't actually be further from the truth of what I now know meditation CAN be. As I've said before, in our busy lives it can be hard to take time out for ourselves as it is - let alone an hour or more to sit in stillness. So be rest assured that it doesn't actually have to take more than 5-10 minutes a day and you can choose to build that up over time (or not) as you want to.

MYTH #2
MEDIATION MEANS SITTING UNCOMFORTABLY ON A COLD FLOOR WITH YOUR LEGS TWISTED INTO LOTUS POSITION

Picture the scene - me and my still-swollen post-baby body willing my puffy legs to cross over each other until I tie myself into a precarious knot. Does that look like peace or bliss? Not so much. Don't worry if you're not flexible enough to sit cross-legged or if the thought of hanging out on the floor gives you hives. You can sit comfortably on a supportive chair or even lie down if you prefer (although this isn't recommended usually as it can be a passport to catching some zzzs. Personally I think falling asleep while you're meditating isn't a cardinal sin, but clearly it does take your mind away from focusing on the here and now so if you think you might doze off while lying down you might be better sitting upright - unless its bedtime, in which case, go right ahead and enjoy the extra blissful rest).

Over time I've become comfortable as a cross-legged floor-sitter (although I credit my yoga practice with that more than my meditation practice) but that's just my personal choice. I do like to sit on the edge of a cushion to push myself slightly forward so my knees touch the ground and I have a stable base - a little tip you might find useful if you find that you hunch your shoulders, lean backwards or feel unbalanced.

But seriously, just sitting comfortably is fine.

MYTH #3
CANDLES, INCENSE AND CHANTING 'OMMM' ARE AN INTEGRAL PART OF MEDITATION

I like a candle as much as the next White Company devotee but unless you find a lit candle particularly soothing or you want to include it as part of a ritual to get you in the mood for your practice, it's totally optional. The same goes for incense, chanting, bells, gongs and mandela beads. They are all perfectly lovely in their own right, and if you find them helpful then that's wonderful, but please don't let not having them delay you from starting your practice.

MYTH #4
MINDFULNESS IS ABOUT CLEAR-ING YOUR MIND OF ALL YOUR THOUGHTS AND ACHIEVING A BLISS-FUL STATE OF NOTHINGNESS.

As I've said, when I first started becoming aware of my thoughts as thoughts, I felt like I was losing my mind rather than discovering it. That crazy tumbling jumble overwhelmed me and I became so frustrated and cross trying to force my mind to be still.

"Just be still, goddammit!" is not the most kind and considerate way to speak to yourself but I found myself reacting that way and getting more and more determined to create the stillness I thought I was meant to be achieving.

In actual fact, our minds are never still. The 86 billion or so brain cells or neurons in our brains fire multiple times every second,[5] sending electrical impulses along our neural pathways like mental superhighways, signalling everything from unconscious actions like parking in our driveway to complex mathematical problems (or completing our tax returns). Our brains are constantly busy, and thinking we can still them by sheer stubbornness is like expecting to be able to stop a waterfall with a spoon.

The a-ha moment for me came when I realised that it wasn't total stillness that I should have been aiming for. It was actually awareness and a release of that busy-ness through learning how to focus on something that was happening right now.

For some people that 'something' is the flicker of a candle, the sound of a syllable repeating, the action of chewing or slow walking or an image that they can concentrate on. For me, that something is my breath.

What I like about using my breath to focus my mind is that it's always with me, always right here in the present moment. Wherever I am, my breath is there too. As I focus on my breathing, noticing how it passes in and out of my body, I'm right here with it, right now.

How my mind tries to sabotage me

So what is my mind doing while I'm concentrating on that in, out, in, out? My mind, in its evolutionary wisdom and base design to be efficient and solve problems, gets distracted from this simple task and so it starts to wander… down the hidden passages of tomorrow it goes, planning supper with Stewart or perhaps hitching a ride in the mental time machine and replaying a memory from yesterday or last week.

These distractions are all just thoughts but it is incredibly easy to get caught up in them, going deeper and deeper down the rabbit hole until we've mentally ordered the whole of this week's grocery order, planned an outfit for that business meeting next month and rewritten history by 'telling' that annoying guy in the queue what we really thought of him.

And here's where meditation practice gets really juicy because at some point, sometimes sooner, sometimes waaaay later, we realise that we've been distracted. And in that moment, in that recognition that what we were doing was thinking instead of noticing our breathing, a beautiful thing happens - awareness.

As well as noticing our breathing, we start to notice our thoughts. And over time that awareness can lead to something very precious and useful - the ability to pause.

I'd like you to imagine a challenging situation that you found yourself in recently - a situation where, very specifically, you reacted to someone else or something else in a way that you now regret.

I'm going to do this right along with you - and I'm going to pick bath time with my two kids a few years ago. This particular evening my son, who was 5-years old, decided for whatever reason that he wasn't going to have a bath and was instead going to ignore me and build the world's longest Lego train in the hallway.

My feelings went from amused to mildly frustrated to downright annoyed. Those emotions flowed through me like a snowball gathering speed down a mountain and led me, ultimately, to shouting at my son to get in the bath. An experience a lot of parents will recognise I'm sure, but not my proudest Mama moment.

Ok, have you got your situation in mind too? What happened? How did you react to that? What exactly were you thinking and feeling as you had that reaction? Can you remember? The chances are you can recall the emotions - anger, frustration, annoyance, rejection, guilt, fear - but not the exact thoughts.

This is because we get caught up in the 'story' and meaning that our mind creates about the situation and we react emotionally to that 'story'. In essence, we react to our thoughts about the situation instead of the situation itself.

Now, let's think back to that awareness and the pause I mentioned as a key benefit of our meditation practice - how might that have helped us in our respective situations?

In my situation it would have been helpful to be aware that I was thinking my son was wilfully disobeying me just to annoy me. If I'd been able to pause for a moment to reflect on the actual truth of that thought before reacting - the truth in this case being that as a five year old he got so incredibly absorbed in what he was doing, he often wouldn't register that I was even speaking to him unless I got down to his level, on my knees, and made eye contact with him - I could have pulled the brakes on that snowball of emotion and made a decision about how to respond rather than reacting.

How about the situation I asked you to recall? What if you'd had awareness of what you were thinking, the story your mind was telling you, the meaning it was creating while you were experiencing your emotions? What if you'd had the ability to pause for a moment before reacting - could you have handled the situation differently? Would you have been happier as a result?

THAT is why I practice thought awareness, through meditating, every day, helping my mind to become more aware. More aware of the here and now, what's going on right at this moment, what my thoughts are, the story that my mind is creating and how that affects my emotions and actions. Not stopping the thoughts, not trying to change them, just being aware of them as they arise, and letting them go.

A SIMPLE 3-STEP MEDITATION PRACTICE

I'd love you to experience the benefits of this for yourself, so to get you started with your own meditation practice try out the 3 simple steps below.

Step #1: Sit comfortably

Find a quiet space somewhere that you won't be disturbed. Unless sitting cross-legged on the floor is comfortable for you, you really don't have to! Simply sit on a supportive chair with your feet flat on the floor and your hands on your knees or in your lap. You can put a small cushion in your lap to support your hands if that's helpful.

Relax your body and try to keep your back as straight as you can. If you find that you clench your jaw or your teeth, it might help to gently place your tongue behind your front teeth.

Set a timer for the amount of time you want to practice - perhaps just 3-5 minutes to start with - so that you don't have to worry about looking at the clock or wondering how long you have left. (Here's a tip: make the alarm sound gentle if you can so it doesn't shock you!)

Step #2: Close your eyes and breathe normally

You don't need to do any special breathing or chant. Just close your eyes and breathe normally.

Listen to the sounds around you so that you become aware of the space you're in. What do you notice? Hold these thoughts lightly and then let them go. Feel the chair or floor under you, your lap or cushion under your hands. Notice these things and then let them go too. We very rarely even think about our immediate surroundings or how our body feels but it can really help you to start off completely grounded in this moment.

Now turn your attention to your breath and just be aware of how the air enters and leaves your body. How does it feel? Where do you notice your breath - in your stomach, your chest? Somewhere else?

In your mind start to count each breath in and each breath out, starting on an in-breath with 1 then following the out-breath with 2 and so on until you reach 10. Then start over. Don't count with too much force, just gently, lightly.

What you might notice quite quickly is how difficult it can be to reach 10 without your thoughts starting to distract you. That's totally fine, natural and expected. Sometimes I get all the way to 50 before I realise my mind is vacationing in the future or hanging out in the past.

Step #3: Watch your thoughts and return to your breath

That voice inside your head? It doesn't mean you're crazy. We all have an internal dialogue that runs in our minds, self-commenting on our day and weaving stories about our experiences.

Remember that mindfulness and meditation isn't about stopping those thoughts or trying to control them, instead it's about watching your thoughts and emotions. When thoughts come along you're just going to practise noticing them without judging or getting caught up in them, but instead seeing them as they are, just thoughts that come and go.

How to deal with thought distraction

This isn't easy, believe me I know! Often our minds are SO scattered they're literally tumbling with thoughts that make us feel like we're drowning, or we can get caught up in a thought stream and lose track of where we are or what we're doing. Please, please be kind to your mind and don't get put off or cross with yourself if this happens.

It's so easy for us to feel like we're failing in some way and then we want to quit. But remember that the point of this practice is exactly that... to just turn up and practice. Try to ditch perfectionism and don't be hard on yourself if the thoughts flow and you find you've latched on to them. Over time you'll become more aware when you've become distracted and learn to guide yourself gently and kindly back to your breathing again.

It is this simple breathing - distraction - awareness - breathing pattern that forms our practice. We're teaching our brain to recognise thoughts as just thoughts, with curiosity and gentleness. If it helps you to be kind to yourself you can try picturing your mind as a young child or animal and gently guiding them back to the breath with a smile.

A helpful guide

Like anything new it can help to have a framework or a guide when you start your mindfulness practice. Once you've tried the simple technique above you might like to experiment with different guided meditations which will walk you through your practice.

My own practice stuttered SO MANY times before I found the guide that was the right 'fit' for me. Give yourself some time to find the practice that works best for you.

Incidentally, my first guide was Andy Puddicombe. He became a monk after a traumatic incident left him questioning his life and he struggled a lot with his own practice, so I knew he felt my pain! (Andy went on to co-create the worldwide meditation project and app, Headspace, to make mindfulness more accessible to everyone.)[6]

**

HABIT #1: REAL LIFE STORY

Zaz (Zarouhi) Grumbar is a yoga teacher practising online at yogawithzaz.com and in person with over 20 years experience and a large following on Instagram where she inspires people to unfurl both their bodies and their minds. She was introduced to thought awareness as the moving, meditative part of her yoga practice but found that awareness transitioned off the mat and helped her to process and interrupt negative thought patterns about her own self-image.

"I remember clearly one day standing in front of the mirror and glancing at my under-arm/side boob fat, running my eyes down over my hips, and just as the words were formulating in my mind to put myself down, another instinct took over. Rather than surrendering to old patterns of thinking, I made a conscious decision to be really aware of my thoughts, and to change the negative narrative. I would make it a game; as soon as the negative me inside was about to speak, I would interrupt with a positive comment - anything at all. "Nice hair today, Zaz" / "I love that your confidence is shining through your eyes" / "You've been through so much, you are a warrior, girl!"

Thought awareness became a constant in Zaz's life, not only as a habit to observe the language and tone she used about herself and to herself but also changing how she thought of other people.

"I felt kinder and more settled. Now, I talk to my students about speaking to ourselves as we would our best friend that we care deeply about."

Zaz is keen to point out that doesn't mean that she doesn't encourage herself to go the extra mile, or to see her faults, but that being intentional about being kind and supportive to herself as an ongoing practice has meant that she no longer tears herself down.

"If I've failed in some way, while I remind myself that I have it in me to do better, to be better, to forgive more - I can also tell myself that I am doing a great job and being the best person I can be in this moment."

MAKE THIS HABIT WORK FOR YOU

- You've got the first building block for your Happiness Habits Transformation - thought awareness. Start using habit #1 and begin your thought awareness practice by setting aside 3-5 minutes each day (or more if you like) in your schedule.
- In your practice time, use the 3-step process above or a guided meditation of your choice. Remember to try not to judge your thoughts as they arise but just to be aware of them and then return to focus on your breathing.
- Be kind to yourself - it's easy to feel discouraged at first if you're constantly distracted! With time you will become more used to dealing with this. In the meantime try placing a suggestion of a smile on your face as you practice to remind you to approach your meditation with curiosity and gentleness.
- Keeping a mindfulness journal can be a great way to see how far you've come with your practice. You can also note down any thoughts that surprised you or were challenging. (If you have a life coach this can be a great basis for discussion.) I've left some space below for you to keep a record of your experiences or make notes in your journal if you'd like to.

YOUR MEDITATION NOTES

"Inspiration is a slender river of brightness leaping from a vast and eternal knowledge."
Sri Aurobindo

CHAPTER FIVE

MY SECOND HAPPINESS HABIT
Why you need to be inspired every day

If you spend time on almost any social media site, you can't fail to have noticed the trend of inspirational quotes being shared. Yes they're motivating, yes they might move you, make you smile or nod. But why is that and why is daily inspiration the second of my happiness habits? We'll discover this and more in this chapter.

In chapter four I talked about how our thoughts direct our emotions and our actions. The internal dialogue that you'll start to become aware of in your thought awareness practice can be a force for positivity or negativity in our day, which is why it's so important for us to start recognising that voice, and encouraging it to work FOR us rather than against us by giving it a focus of its own.

When daily inspiration shifts that focus it can be the fire that sparks an intention for our whole day. And if that intention is positive and motivating it can drive us forward to do amazing things!

My own experience of inspiration started in my teenage years. When I was fifteen years old a new English teacher started at my school. Ms Howard was tall and slim, her straight dark brown hair was flecked with silver and her mind was as sharp as a razor. I loved her instantly. She was the first woman, outside of my family, to truly inspire me. It's partly thanks to her that you have this book in your hands, I suppose, as she cemented the love of writing I always had as a child into a passion that kept me up late into the night completing assignments with a fervour my other subjects never benefited from.

One of the things that inspired me most about Ms Howard was that teaching wasn't her first profession - she was also a barrister. Sometimes she would be away from school for a few days, busy working with her clients or at court, and I remember how much this impressed me. I remember thinking how brilliant it was that she was so talented, she could have more than one job and still have time to personally inspire each of us in the classroom to be the best that we could be.

The 'tricky' boys in the class soon realised that her courtroom experience and wordsmithery also made her the master of the amiable put down. They begrudgingly accepted her, before, I believe, coming to admire her as much as I did.

Ms Howard was able to do something remarkable; she looked into each one of us and saw a potential that we didn't yet see in ourselves. She opened the door to opportunity for some, to imagination for others and to endless possibility for me.

When she left the school a year or so later I was devastated but I never forgot the mark she left on me - the mark of inspiration.

So what really is inspiration? According to the dictionary definition, to inspire is to "fill with the urge or ability to do or feel something," but for me it's so much more than that.

Inspiration is possibility, it's courage, it's opportunity and excitement. It's the spark that lights a flame within us, firing our imagination, fuelling our passions and purpose.

Inspiration can come in many forms, but it has these qualities that touch us deeply and motivate us to take action. Memorable quotes for example can have a power way beyond the sum of their words. Think of great leaders and their memorable sound bites, like former US President Barack Obama's "Yes We Can" which moved audiences to yell at the top of their voices and acted as a catalyst for his entire political campaign.

But why do these sound bites resonate so deeply with us? While some truly inspiring words stand the test of time - such as Horace's famous "Carpe Diem" which means making the most of the present time, and literally translates as "seize the day" - often quotes that touch us today may not work the same way next month or next year. Our reaction to them depends on where we are in our lives, our emotional state or receptiveness.

At a primal level, we're all aspirational. Psychologist Isaac Maslow believed there is a set of needs that we all move through as part of our journey from survival to flourishing. As we move through this 'hierarchy of needs'[7] from the basic physiological requirements of food, water and sex to more complex psychological desires like self-confidence and self-achievement, we often gravitate towards teachers or role models who can help us to go further, faster.

Ms Howard was one such role model for me, and I'm inspired by other amazing women, like Audrey Hepburn, Maya Angelou, Amelia Earhart and Oprah Winfrey, who challenge societal norms or break the boundaries of their past to create real change and beauty in the world.

Look through the autobiographies of famous entrepreneurs, actors, politicians, leaders and change makers and you'll likely find inspirational figures that galvanised something deep within them and encouraged them to go beyond where they thought they should be to where they truly could be.

The entrepreneur, philanthropist and life and business strategist Tony Robbins has credited motivational speaker and author Jim Rohn as one of his major inspirations. Robbins met Rohn when Rohn was about 50, and Tony was just 17. "He was a beautiful man," Robbins says, who taught him "happiness and success in life are not the result of what we have, but rather of how we live and what we do with the things we have makes the biggest difference in the quality of life."[8] And in her book "What I Know For Sure", Oprah Winfrey writes that a paragraph in Gary Zukav's book "The Seat of the Soul" was life-changing for her.[9]

Inspirational words help us to recognise something within ourselves that we want to change and motivate us to seek out ways to make those changes.

Above all, it's encouraging to read a book or quote, watch a video or listen to a piece of music that makes us feel like someone else is on our side. And this is even more powerful if they have (or we believe they have) experienced something similar to what we're going through, and succeeded in overcoming challenges along the way.

Why? Because it tells our mind "they can do it, so perhaps I can too" just as if someone is coaching and motivating us to improve.

When I was struggling to find my way as a new mother I started reading parenting blogs, gaining solace in the knowledge that I wasn't the only one struggling with post-natal depression, parenthood and trying to make a living. But I realised that when I read more aspirational blogs, those that attracted me because they were a step ahead of where I was, rather than battling away in the trenches like me, my outlook was much more positive. I realised that in order to lift myself I needed to be lifted, to draw strength from the achievements of others who had come before me, to be inspired by their stories and motivated to work for my own achievements. Literally, 'positive in, positive out'.

Eventually I started my own blog, documenting my journey and offering tips and advice that I'd found helpful, hoping to perhaps in some way inspire others as I'd been inspired myself, and pay forward that mental and emotional 'lift'.

And ultimately in my coaching practice that's what I did too, opening up my client's minds to the possibilities that lie within them, inspiring them to become the best version of themselves that they can possibly imagine and motivating them to go beyond their self-perceived boundaries to live their ideal lives now.

But you don't need a coach to benefit from inspiration. Quotes, books, scripture, music, art, podcasts, videos - all these things can inspire and motivate us. And of course inspiration can be different things for different people.

Vicki Broadbent, author of Mumboss/The Working Mom and founder of award-winning blog HonestMum. com, finds inspiration in different ways:

"I tend to find inspiration in the everyday as a busy blogger, author and mum of three and it's these real-life events I document frequently and which seem to connect with my audience the most (being relatable, universal experiences) spanning birth stories, parenting challenges and wins; my experience of balancing a creative career with raising kids and beyond. Writing and filmmaking is how I make sense of the world around me. I've learned to be open and somewhat vulnerable online to help others - to candidly share the bad times with the good.

I find thinking of my end user and whom I can help with my work, unlocks my confidence and keeps me continuously sharing. My readers inspire me as much as I them, and it's their messages which encourage me. I also actively seek out inspiration on a daily basis, reading and watching what interests me, as well as consuming content outside of the usual genres I enjoy. This also helps if I find I'm creatively blocked in some way. I let the arts re-inspire me whether that's viewing a new exhibition, attending a creative workshop or painting myself. Taking time out of my busy schedule and prioritising self-care is also vital to the process. You have to live life in order to write about life. That time and space switching off provides time to reflect and create art without pressure. It's then, the magic happens. I'm always more productive after a break".

Do we have to wait for inspiration to strike us to benefit from it? When we picture inspiration it's often like a lightning bolt appearing out of the sky, but I believe that, as Vicki says, we can actively seek out inspiration and pull it into our daily lives.

I've made it part of my daily routine to read, watch or listen to something inspiring every day. That inspiration directs my focus towards positivity, lifts my mood, encourages and motivates me to move forward in the right direction with the right mindset to achieve my goals.

So let's see what it can do for you, shall we?

Here's a three-step process for bringing daily inspiration, my second Happiness Habit, into your life:

Step one: Who inspires you?

We're all different when it comes to who inspires us. Thought leaders, spiritual leaders, celebrities, historical figures, artists, poets, entrepreneurs, authors, film stars, musicians... only you can decide who inspires you.

Perhaps it's someone who's been through a situation you're going through and overcome challenges you're facing, a historical figure whose life story encourages you to reach out your hand and stretch for your most exciting dreams, a figure from your past who inspired you at a young age or a religious or spiritual teacher who embodies a feeling that you want to welcome into your own life.

Don't worry if you don't have anyone in mind yet, discovering your own personal sources of inspiration is a wonderful journey of exploration and bear in mind that this can change over time too as you grow and your circumstances change.

Take some time to think about *who* or *what* inspires you, *why* they inspire you and make some notes below or in your journal.

Step two: How do you like to be inspired?

As well as knowing who or what inspires us, it's useful to think about how we want to receive that inspiration. For some a YouTube video can drive them to start a business, for others a podcast can fill them with ideas they're itching to move forward on, while for others reading a book or bible passage inspires them to be the best they can be that day. Or perhaps art or quotes inspire you?

Think about the different ways that you like to be inspired and make some notes about them below or in your journal.

Step three: find your inspiration sources and add them into your daily routine.

Using your answers from steps one and two, search out your own personal sources of inspiration. They will become the special forces you can call on when you need a dash of motivation or a splash of creativity.

One of my favourite inspirational books is "What I Know For Sure" by Oprah Winfrey - I literally read it from cover to cover and then go back to the beginning and start again!

I've added a list of motivating books and podcasts below - if you're stuck for ideas take a look and see if any of these work for you. But I also encourage you to seek out your own as well and add them into your daily inspiration habit.

INSPIRING BOOKS

- Anthony Robbins: "Awaken the giant within"
- Oprah Winfrey: "What I Know For Sure"
- Brené Brown: "The gifts of imperfection"
- Jim Rohn: "The art of exceptional living"
- Maya Angelou: "I know why the caged bird sings"
- Dr Wayne Dyer: "Change your thoughts, change your life"
- Gary Zukav: "The seat of the soul"
- Dr Norman Vincent Peal: "The power of positive thinking"
- Richard Wiseman: "60 seconds - change your life in under a minute"
- Nick Vujicic: "Life without limits"
- Susan Jeffers: "Feel the fear and do it anyway"
- Zig Ziglar: "Better than good"
- Victor E Frankl: "Man's search for meaning"
- Jack Canfield & Mark Victor Hanson: "Chicken soup for the soul"
- Robin Sharma: "The monk who sold his Ferrari"
- Deepak Choprah: "The 7 spiritual laws of success"
- Anne Frank: "The Diary of Anne Frank"
- Martha Beck: "Steering by Starlight"
- Brendon Burchard: "The Motivation Manifesto"
- Vicki Broadbent: "Mumboss"/"The Working Mom"
- Marie Forleo: "Everything is Figureoutable"

PODCASTS

- Magic Lessons and The Good Life Project - with Elizabeth Gilbert
- The Lively Show - with Jess Lively
- This Is My Era: The Podcast
- The Brendon Show - with Brendon Burchard
- Kwik Brain - with Jim Kwik
- Oprah's Master Class: The Podcast
- The Shift (On Life After 40) - with Sam Baker
- Achieve Your Goals - with Hal Elrod
- The Robcast - with Rob Bell
- How to Wow - with Chris Evans

***

HABIT #2: REAL LIFE STORY

Julie Brown is a visibility and media coach at iamjuliebrown.com working with female coaches and consultants to increase their impact, credibility and attract more clients.

When she worked as a busy editor for national publications, Julie had no shortage of creative people to tap into when she needed inspiration. So when she became self-employed, spending hours in her office on her own, things felt a bit different. "Yes, I'm a creative person but even the most creative of us need a shot of inspiration from time to time," she says.

"I help my clients with inspiration and motivation on a daily basis, but like a lot of things in life we don't always practice what we preach. For me working from a café, co-working space or beach (Brighton in my case) can be hugely inspirational; all that people-watching and chatting to do."

But when the global pandemic and restrictions of lockdown hit, Julie soon realised she'd have to find a new source of inspiration - and the one she found was quite unexpected.

"This is when I found my tree of inspiration. OK it sounds weird I know, but they say that trees are good for the soul, and writers, philosophers and even politicians have found inspiration in the branches and leaves around them. Research has now identified that spending time in a forest simply looking at trees reduces stress and forest bathing has become popular across the globe. During the first UK lockdown in March 2020 I'd taken to sitting on one of the benches in our village graveyard to look out over the Sussex Downs. It was so peaceful during a time of so much chaos."

It was on one of these visits that Julie noticed the tree.

"I have no idea why it grabbed my attention - just one of many trees in the graveyard. This was early-April so it didn't have any leaves, but there was just something about it. Tall, wide and solid and if I didn't know differently, I'd say wise too. Now it's worth pointing out here that I'm one of the least 'woo-woo' people you could ever meet. I'm more of a straightforward and direct kinda gal. So, I can't explain it, but I simply felt compelled to have a feel of this tree. A little wander around it is all I needed, then I left."

And that was it. She'd found her new source of inspiration. And it turns out, this isn't that unusual. Julie has since met a few people who have 'special' trees they visit regularly.

Now Julie has transformed her inspiring tree visits into a regular habit in her routine.

"I make a point of visiting the tree as often as I can. It's a self-care thing. A way to start the day positively or a moment to look forward to. Sometimes, I just wander up there, take a few deep breaths and sit for a minute before heading home to work. Or I may take my computer along to do some planning or writing. But mostly I use the time with my tree to reflect and be inspired. The calmness I feel when I'm there helps me clear my head, allowing in the creative thoughts I need to do my work effectively. Even if I'm feeling stressed or under the weather when I get there, I'm soon restored to my usual self. The scenery, with my tree in the middle of it all is stunning. It's time for myself. A bit of mindfulness."

MAKE THIS HABIT WORK FOR YOU:

- You've got your second transformational habit - daily inspiration. Find the right sources of inspiration for you using the 3-step process above and keep them somewhere that you can refer to them each day, on your desk or by your nightstand for example.
- Schedule some time each morning for your daily inspiration (it doesn't need to take more than 10minutes but add more if you'd like to) and block it out in your planner or calendar.
- Switch off or mute your phone so that you're not distracted and open your mind to being inspired.
- Capture any ideas or reflections that come to mind in the space below or keep a notebook or journal to hand. I often find this is one of my most productive times for ideas!

YOUR NOTES

*"Enjoy the little things, for one day you may look back
and realise they were the big things."*
Robert Brault

CHAPTER SIX

MY THIRD HAPPINESS HABIT
*Cultivating an attitude of gratitude
and practising it every day*

Gratitude. It's become quite the buzzword, credited with everything from making you happier to relieving stress. But why is that, why did it become my third happiness habit, and how can we cultivate an attitude of gratitude in our hectic lives?

I know that recording what I'm grateful for as part of my morning routine, first thing before I get caught up in my inbox, actions or the drama of family life, creates a positive feeling that lingers throughout the day.

And I'm not alone. Scientific studies have looked at the effects of gratitude and found real tangible benefits.

Robert A Emmons, Ph.D., a leading researcher in the field of gratitude, conducted a study in 2003 and found that people who kept gratitude journals on a weekly basis felt better about their lives as a whole, were more optimistic about the week ahead, were more likely to have made progress towards their personal goals and even exercised more regularly.[10]

Brené Brown, Ph.D., LMSW, writer and research professor at The University of Houston noted the link between gratitude and joy in her own research, finding that every person she interviewed who described themselves as joyful, actively practised gratitude on a regular basis.[11]

And the good news is it's not age dependent - in another study, children who practised grateful thinking had more positive attitudes toward school and their families.[12] So this is a habit the whole family can benefit from.

WHY GRATITUDE CAN BE CHALLENGING

But what if you don't feel naturally grateful? For some of us, it can be hard to find those moments of gratitude while for others it comes more easily.

Robert A Emmons, Ph.D. and Robin S. Stern, Associate Director of the Yale Center for Emotional Intelligence note that people with a grateful personality are more likely to experience more joy, love and enthusiasm. And at the same time they are more easily protected from destructive emotions like envy, greed and bitterness.[13]

Some people may be more predisposed to be grateful than others, but starting and, importantly, practising a *habit* of gratitude can actually bring the same effects over time.

I know this because my natural tendency is to come from a

place of scarcity and focus on the small negative moments of my day rather than seeing the bigger picture, so I've had to train myself to shift that focus to the broader positives in my life.

That place of scarcity is somewhere I became very familiar with in my business too. I've worked with clients who literally couldn't see the amazing life they were living every day. Without the perspective of a wider view they focussed in on the details of the things they hadn't achieved, didn't own or hadn't experienced.

And I've carried my own passport to that place, seeing only the negativity in my day and completely missing the beauty that surrounds it.

When my daughter was young and struggling to sleep for more than a few hours at a time, I honed in on that detail. I lamented my own lack of rest and forgot that I'd finally gotten what I'd been wishing for years for; a healthy baby girl. Shifting into that wider viewpoint meant being actively grateful for what I did have rather than what I didn't. It was a lesson I learned then, but I continue to remind myself of it in my daily gratitude practice even now.

When we're not practising gratitude it's easy to approach life from that place of scarcity, anxiety and vulnerability. Our natural tendency and ability to compare ourselves with others (now right at the tip of our smartphone-ready fingers) can lead us to feel inadequate; we're not thin enough, fat enough, smart enough, wealthy enough, strong enough, fit enough, pretty enough, popular enough… the list is endless.

From gym memberships and beauty products to the culture of endless education and credential-collecting, whole industries rely on us feeling 'less than'. Now, don't get me wrong, I'm not saying that personal development isn't important or useful, quite the contrary, as a coach I was part of that industry myself. But the key here, in my opinion, is to approach personal development as a growth opportunity, to learn and evolve, rather than to keep up with The Joneses or as a stick to beat yourself up with.

The fact is that there will always be someone wealthier than you, thinner than you, younger than you, more experienced than you. Focusing on what we do have rather than what we don't doesn't mean we shouldn't have dreams or goals - but it does allow us to have that sense of perspective that gratitude brings and gives us the opportunity to set those goals without a scarcity mindset.

GRATITUDE AND INVITING DISASTER

When I was coming out of the black days of my depression, I became very aware of my language. I realised, with no small shock, that there were days when almost everything that I said or thought was negative in some way.

If the sun was shining I'd worry about it being too hot. If I tried making a new dish for my daughter to try, I'd tell Stewart that I didn't expect her to eat it. If someone said something flattering to me I'd tell myself they were just being nice, that they didn't really mean it. If I lost 2lb I'd be certain to put it back on again by the weekend.

This negativity, I came to realise, was a defence mechanism against disappointment. If I never expected a positive outcome, I couldn't be let down. It was as if in some way by being optimistic I was inviting disaster.

Because I'd cultivated the habit of negativity, at first I had a resistance to practising gratitude for the same reason.

"If I'm grateful for something in my life, it might get taken away from me!"

You'd think that with all the blessings in my life it would be easy to see the positive in almost any situation, but I was so anxious in my vulnerability with an overpowering desire to maintain control, that I built a wall around my heart preventing any joy from my here-and-now from getting in.

I was, by definition, a defensive pessimist for years, and while I still have to check myself when that mechanism starts to seep into my life, undoubtedly practising gratitude every day has helped me to break down that wall, allowing me to experience the pure joy of life unfolding around me.

GRATITUDE AND COMPARISONITIS

There's a famous quote - "Comparison is the thief of joy" (attributed usually to President Theodore Roosevelt or author Dwight Edwards) but it's also the thief of gratitude.

It's actually completely normal to wonder how we compare to other people. And there's nothing wrong with it per se. In psychological terms, this drive is part of our basic desire to understand ourselves and our place in the social world. This was really important when we lived in caves and as part of tribes as we needed to know where we stood. At that time if we were all throwing ourselves about, wanting to lead the tribe there would be lots of fighting and not enough surviving!

We're not in survival mode anymore but that drive still exists within us and it's often triggered by our thoughts. If our self-worth and self-confidence are low or our self-doubt is high we are more likely to look outside of ourselves for a comparison. We try to validate our view of ourselves. How good or bad am I?

The thoughts we then have about the gap created by that comparison and the meaning we create can be positive ("If they can do this, so can I!") or negative ("I'll never be as good as them!")

When those thoughts are negative they can often spiral, leaving us feeling very negatively about ourselves and the person we were comparing with... even if we don't even know them!

"Who does she think she is anyway? I never liked her..."

Let's take another example, a lady, let's call her Sarah, wants to lose weight but she's struggling to reach her goal and feels bad about that. She sees another woman every day on her way to work who is very thin and Sarah compares herself with her. Even if she doesn't know any more about her, Sarah might tell herself…

"I bet she eats more healthily than me"
"I bet she goes to the gym every day unlike me"
"I bet she's happier than me"

Sarah has created a whole story about the other woman based just on what she sees. But what Sarah can't see is the TRUTH from the other woman's perspective.

Perhaps she has a chronic illness that prevents her from putting on weight… perhaps she has IBS and has a very restricted diet… perhaps she has a high metabolism… perhaps she was anorexic as a teenager because her Mother told her every day that she was fat and now she struggles to eat normally… or perhaps she does eat healthily and exercise regularly.

The point is Sarah doesn't know. And we often don't know the other side of the story when we compare ourselves with others, do we?

"The reason we struggle with insecurity is because we compare our behind-the-scenes with everyone else's highlight reel."
Steven Furtick, pastor and author

This is where Sarah gets to make a choice (even if she doesn't realise it yet). If she responds positively to the story she has created, she can use the other woman as a source of inspiration and make a commitment to sticking to her own goals by using her as a role model without ever knowing more about her.

But if she responds negatively, seeing the story through a filter of her own lack of confidence, she might feel bad about herself, feel like quitting and even resent the other woman for having something that she doesn't have. Hello scarcity.

Being in that scarcity mindset means that we feel like because someone else has something, we can't have it, as though there isn't enough to go around and they've taken our share. It's no wonder we can feel envy and resentment as a result!

And, as with defensive pessimism, when we compare, we shift our focus away from what we have, what we've accomplished, what we can be rightly and justly grateful for.

MAKING GRATITUDE PART OF YOUR ROUTINE AND OVERCOMING RESISTANCE

When I started adding moments of gratitude into my week it felt good to be seeing the positive from time to time. But it wasn't until I made it a regular practice, every single day that I really began to see the benefits.

We become what we regularly do and by making gratitude part of my Happiness Habits Transformation, as with all the habits I'm sharing with you in this book, I started intentionally shifting my attitude on a daily basis. I was actively training my mind to see the glass half full rather than half empty, stolen by someone or not there at all!

As a recovering defensive pessimist this was a BIG deal for me.

Of course, it isn't easy some days, when the morning starts with a sleepless night, the kids are spitting fire at each other, and all that lands in my inbox is bills. So on days when I'm struggling to see the silver lining on my clouds, I start small and use my senses.

On those tricky days, or if I start to fall into a pattern with what I'm feeling grateful for, I use this four-step exercise to freshen up my gratitude by getting specific.

Step one: Be present here and now

Stop what you're doing and focus on what you can see, smell, touch, taste or hear.

It could be the sun shining through a cloud and highlighting a bird on a branch in the garden; the smell of coffee brewing in the kitchen; the touch of a soft scarf around your neck; the taste of a crisp cold apple; the ticking of the clock on the wall.

Step two: Appreciate

Whatever it is that catches your attention, say to yourself:

"right here, right now I have something to be grateful for."

Step three: Past & Future

Now that you've shifted your attitude, try to broaden your focus out a little and find two other things that you can be grateful for - one in the past and one in the future.

Step Four: Make a record

Write down the three things you're grateful for and why you feel that way. If you want to try this exercise now, you can make some notes below or in your journal.

Ok, I hear you asking, but what about when times are REALLY tough?

It can be easy to practise gratitude when life is going well; when the sun is shining, your child's report card is good, and your business is bringing in new clients left and right.

But what about when life is really tough? What about those days when it feels like nothing is going right? When the guilt kicks in and we just feel like throwing in the towel and running off to a beach somewhere for a moment's peace (and margaritas).

Here's the thing, it's important to remember that bad things will always happen. We cannot control every area of our lives but we can control how we *react* to what happens in our lives.

And it's our attitude that helps to frame those reactions.

An attitude of gratitude, practised regularly, can help us to trust that goodness exists, even when the poop is hitting the proverbial fan.

By adding a moment of reflection and appreciation into our daily routine we're priming that attitude of gratitude. Flexing its muscles if you like. So that when times ARE tough, it's ready and waiting for us to call on it to help us frame our reactions in the most positive way that we can.

It's all about perspective and reminding ourselves that nothing is permanent, that everything passes with time.

It's really important to record what you're grateful for by writing it down. Writing helps to organise our thoughts and the action of putting pen to paper (or finger to keyboard) cements all that positive energy in our minds.

I write my gratitude list in my planner so that I see it throughout the day, but you may prefer to use a notebook or a specific gratitude journal.

In The Flourish Handbook, Cheryl Rickman; author, ghostwriter and social activist, suggests creating a gratitude board to display on your wall. "Gather photographs, pictures, words that provide a snapshot of moments, things, people, experiences you are grateful for."

However you choose to capture your daily gratitude practice, there will be times when, for whatever reason, you struggle to see the silver lining or when you can't think of anything unique about that particular day. So here are some gratitude prompts that you can use to stimulate your own thoughts.

GRATITUDE PROMPTS

Home, family, relationships

- ▶ Is there a room in your home that you particularly love or a keepsake that has special memories for you?
- ▶ Is there a moment with your kids or other family members in the last week that was very special, or made you smile?

- ▶ Does your partner do something to help you that you maybe overlook sometimes?
- ▶ Is there a moment recently that you and your partner shared that made you both laugh?
- ▶ What first attracted you to your partner that you can still see in them today?
- ▶ Is there a special friend that's there for you, on the end of the phone/social media ready for a chat or when you want to rant?

Work

- ▶ Is there someone at work that's always ready to lend a hand if you need it?
- ▶ What makes you feel good at work... donuts on Friday, free coffee/tea, great smelling soap in the bathroom?
- ▶ Was there a moment in your day at work this week where you nailed something you've been working on?
- ▶ Did you see something on the way to work that made you smile?
- ▶ Did you read or listen to something on your commute yesterday that lifted your mood or made you think?
- ▶ Have you challenged yourself in your business this week and stepped out of your comfort zone?
- ▶ Did someone say something nice about your team, work, or attitude?

- ▶ Is there a special event coming up at work that you're looking forward to?

The world around us / general

- ▶ What do you see when you look out of your window? Name one thing that is beautiful or reminds you that nature is amazing.
- ▶ Is the sun shining? Is the rain creating a rainbow? (Even in a storm we can be grateful to be indoors!)
- ▶ Can you hear a bird singing if you close your eyes?
- ▶ Can you hear your house heating rumbling away, keeping you warm?
- ▶ Is there something in your fridge that you're looking forward to eating?
- ▶ How many things can you see around you that are your favourite colour?
- ▶ Have you read a book or seen a film recently that made you smile or think?
- ▶ What holiday are you looking forward to the most this year? Why?
- ▶ What favourite item of clothing makes you feel great when you wear it?

***

HABIT #3: REAL LIFE STORY

George Bentley, UK Managing Director of ThinkSmart Software Ltd, a global company providing world class software to thousands of children's activity providers, knows from personal experience how easy it is to be so tied up with busy-ness, focusing on the wrong things, that we completely forget the good that is going on around us.

"I was letting the small wins get swallowed up by the big losses. Many times, I'd catch myself talking about what didn't go well in the week and how I needed to improve the following week. I've always been very goal driven and when I had something to aim for, I gave it everything. When I didn't reach a certain goal, whether that be signing a new client, winning a tennis match, or releasing a new feature in our software, I'd be feeling disappointed. I'd spend the weekend strategizing in my head and working out why I hadn't reached my goal.

My wife, Sarah, would know almost the second I walked through the door whether I'd had a stressful day or wasn't happy with a particular result. She has and always will be very understanding but I always felt more frustrated when someone else could see I was disappointed or stressed with a certain outcome. This resulted in me switching off less as my mind was engulfed in what I could do better and what I didn't do well enough. This wasn't healthy."

It took an early morning walk with a close friend, Kieran, for George to realise that everyone can change how they interpret results and how they view the world around them.

"Kieran was always gripping hold of the positives in his life and not the negatives. I was in awe of the gratitude he possessed daily. It looked a lot healthier than dwelling on what wasn't going well. I decided it was time to go on a journey. I needed to change the way I was summarising my week and find the positives. The small wins were there, and I just needed to find them. It's amazing how many are there that we simply overlook. I knew there were multiple ways to express gratitude, but I needed to find a way that worked for me. That way was writing them down. Things always feel more real for me when I write them down. I can see them, and I can feel the gratitude seeping out as I put pen to paper.

It was amazing how many small wins I was grateful for daily. It was also worrying how many I simply ignored without knowing. I enjoyed sharing my newfound wins with Sarah and showing her what I was grateful for. She's always smiling and thinking positively but even she had forgotten some of the things that happened during the week.

Everyone who practises this habit will probably have their own way of doing it. For me, I do it once per week and on a Monday morning. I've tried doing it daily, every other day etc but the fact of the matter is that this format works for me. I'm consistent with it. Every Monday morning, I open my notepad and have a specific section in which I write everything I'm grateful for from the week before. I love starting my week and listing every small win from the week before. I often catch Sarah reading through it and I love the smile on her face after seeing what I'm grateful for (she appears in the list frequently). I remember the lovely meals Sarah may have cooked, a book I've finished reading, how someone made me feel, seeing staff interact with each other, a phone call with my family, a software problem that caused the team stress but that was resolved quickly. My lists are always random but everything on the list has been a small win in my eyes."

Once George had practised this habit for about three months, he noticed a change in himself.

"I was approaching situations differently and looking for more of the positives rather than the negatives. I now handle stressful situations differently and this has resulted in better communication between myself, my team and those closest to me. It's not just me either. I've noticed people in my life looking for more of the positives when the chips are down.

During a difficult time for the world these past 2 years, I still found myself looking for the small wins. At one point, our company was losing a lot of money, my staff were struggling, my friends were furloughed, and I didn't have a clue what the future held. My gratitude list ensured I stayed strong mentally and looked for the smallest of wins during the hardest time of my career to date. And that, I am grateful for!"

MAKE THIS HABIT WORK FOR YOU

- You've got your third Happiness Habit - daily gratitude. Try adding a gratitude moment into your daily
  routine. Put it on your schedule to remind you or set
  an alarm on your phone for the same time every day.
- I like to practise gratitude first thing in the morning
  after habits #1 #2 and #4 but others like to do it just
  before they go to bed. Experiment by slotting it into
  your day (or week) when it works best for you and
  refine it as you go along.
- Write down three things that you're grateful for -
  whatever has most meaning for you. You can use
  the present, past and future exercise or the gratitude
  prompts if you like.
- Record what you're grateful for in the space below or
  in your journal.

MY GRATITUDE NOTES

"Take care of your body.
It's the only place you have to live."
Jim Rohn

CHAPTER SEVEN

MY FOURTH HAPPINESS HABIT
Make moving your body your daily stress
solution without joining a gym

If we're honest we all know the benefits of exercise. From reducing our risk of heart disease, stroke, type 2 diabetes, high blood pressure, and some cancers to strengthening our bones and muscles. It's all good.

It's also a great de-stressor, builds your confidence, helps you think more clearly, increases your energy, and releases those gorgeous endorphins that boost your mood for hours after you've worked out.

But as a busy working mother I know from experience how hard it can be to find the time AND the motivation to exercise.

After our kids came along I used to think that the only way I'd exercise every morning was if someone was there to pull me out of bed, drag me to the exercise mat and stand shouting at me to get it done! (That's totally a thing you can pay for, by the way.)

This is surprising because being active was something my Father instilled in me at an early age. He was a black belt in the martial art Shotokan Karate and loved the guy-camaraderie of lifting weights at the gym. I remember watching him practising his 'katas' or boxing a punch bag in our basement, wanting to join in and trying my tiny hands in his huge boxing gloves. I also remember him teaching me to defend myself using his karate techniques (something I've only ever had to do once, thankfully).

Fast forward to my teenage years and my mother and I would bounce along to her Jane Fonda Workout video in the living room, decked out in our 80s gear (complete with maroon leg warmers), feeling 'the burn'.

I wasn't particularly good at sports at school, I liked netball and hockey but cross country and athletics left me cold. It wasn't until two enthusiastic ladies started running aerobics classes in the local village hall, that I officially got the exercise 'bug'. While their names are lost in the mists of time I remember the way they looked vividly - one, let's call her Fiona, was tall and slim with straight brown hair and a confident, beaming smile that lit up the room. The other, we'll call her Linda, was shorter and a little pumper, with bouncy blonde curls and a wicked sense of humour. I loved them both and couldn't wait for their classes each week.

The combination of pumping tunes and moves with these ladies' infectious energy was as thrilling to me as an evangelist speaker and I progressed slowly from the back, week by week as I improved, learning the routines and finally making it to the coveted front row, reserved for the keenest and most experienced participants.

Fiona and Linda started using me as an example in class for other group members to follow and I arrived a few minutes early some weeks to chat and get to know them better. Eventually one day they asked if I wanted to try leading part of the class myself - not strictly allowed I now know - but I jumped at the chance, and they taught me how to mirror, cue and teach their routines. My confidence soared. I felt like I'd found my place, my groove, and although I never went on to gain any fitness qualifications, my love of exercise (and public speaking) really blossomed from there.

Why am I telling you this? Not just because being active helped me lose my teenage baby-fat and change my body shape, although it did, or because it kept me fit and healthy, although it did and still does, but because it made me FEEL incredible. It boosted my confidence, gave me goals to aim for and achievements to be proud of. I even met my husband at a fitness class that he happened to be running outside of his day job because he shared my love of the fitness 'buzz'.

But here's the thing. Depression has a way of depleting your energy and making you forget the things you love. And it took me some time, and considerable effort, after my daughter was born to make myself start moving my body again. It felt like too much of a struggle, too hard, I didn't have the time… I used every excuse to put it off. .

But when I finally did start exercising again I realised how amazing it made me feel both in my body AND my mind.

Dr Juliet McGrattan; author of "Sorted: The Active Women's Guide to Health", blogger, runner and former GP, explains why;

"People often think that exercise does our body good by helping us control our weight, and lose a few pounds if we need to. Whilst this is true, exercise also has an anti-inflammatory action in the body, crucial for our physical and mental wellbeing. In terms of mental health, exercise can help to reduce the risk of depression and dementia and the power that exercise has to lift mood, build self-esteem, energise and invigorate us, should not be underestimated. The release of endorphins that occurs when we exercise brings a sense of wellbeing and sometimes after vigorous, prolonged exercise, a feeling of euphoria. We have this wonderful reserve of natural 'feel good chemicals' just waiting to be used. Building a regular exercise habit can have a dramatic effect, not only on our performance but also on our outlook on life."

And that's why moving my body daily became one of my Happiness Habits. Not out of punishment, or obligation, but out of a commitment to myself to make time for something that makes me feel good and brings me joy. Now that I'm almost fifty I usually use that time to focus on weight training to support my bones but even when my writing and being around for my kids and family means I have a tight schedule, I still try to make sure that I include at least ten-twenty minutes of exercise in my routine every day.

I do it first thing so I know that it's done and I can get on with my day. I'll also join a yoga class with friends when I can, and I make a point to walk or cycle at the weekend, listening to a favourite podcast or audiobook.

That's how I make it work for me.

Now, if you're reading this, cringing at the thought of lycra shorts and rooms of sweaty people jumping up and down, and thinking there's no way you can build exercise into your busy day, please bear with me. I'm not suggesting that you sign up for the London Marathon or even join a gym.

There are lots of ways to incorporate movement into our daily lives and I've listed 50 different suggestions for you at the end of this chapter. But first let's look at what else might be stopping you...

When I asked a group of busy women why they didn't exercise regularly, not having the time was one of the main reasons.

But you don't actually have to move your body for hours to get some gorgeous benefits. The World Health Organisation recommends that at least 150 minutes of moderate intensity exercise a week is enough to keep you fit and healthy[14] - that's about 20 minutes a day but, importantly, it doesn't have to be done all at once.

And while the immediate positive psychological effects of exercise are a great bonus, research has shown 20 minutes of exercise a day can also boost your mood for hours afterwards.[15] But even ten minutes can have a positive effect when you're first starting out - ten minutes is better than zero minutes, after all. (In fact there are specific exercise routines that focus entirely on shorter periods of time like the Tabata and Gibala high intensity training systems.) And no matter how busy your life is, I'm betting you can find ten short movement moments in your day.

In fact, aside from setting dedicated time for moving your body, if you look at the rest of your day you'll probably find that you're already moving more than you think you are - walking to meetings, as part of your commute or to and from school, gardening, going up and down the stairs at home or work - every little helps so try to make a point of maximising this time.

I know this can all sound really daunting if exercise isn't even on the agenda yet for you, so I have some pain-free, simple solutions to get you started.

But first let's tackle some other reasons why we just don't move our bodies enough...

"Why can't I just work out once a week?"

Of course once a week is better than nothing but health professionals recommend that we move our bodies every day. Plus you'll start seeing the positive benefits of daily exercise that go beyond how you look and impact how you feel too. And you'll have those benefits every day rather than just once a week.

"I'm too tired, I just don't get enough sleep."

I hear you on this one! And if you have a newborn, you're breastfeeding or suffering from an illness, there will absolutely be days when you should reserve your energy. But apart from that, as long as your doctor has given you the all clear, exercising regularly will actually give you more energy to get through your day.[16]

You don't need to be doing anything too taxing either to start off with - gentle stretches and building up to a few yoga poses will still boost your mood and make you feel a sense of achievement for prioritising you. Then when you feel ready you can progress to more strenuous exercise at your own pace - ultimately you're aiming to raise your heart rate with moderate-intensity aerobic physical activity and some muscle strengthening exercises.

"I hate going to the gym."

If you've got the time but you hate the gym, don't let that stop you! There are lots of ways that you can move your body without going to the gym. Do you like doing things in a group? See if there are some local walking or jogging groups, join a sports team or a dance or yoga class.

Prefer exercising on your own? Try swimming, running, walking, yoga videos, gardening, dancing in front of the TV even. If you have kids you can get them involved too (we often have a Friday night dance-off in the kitchen!) Check out the list coming up for lots more ideas.

"I've tried before."

If you're struggling to get motivated when something hasn't worked before, it can help to consider why it didn't work last time - did you pick an exercise you didn't enjoy? Did you set yourself goals for your exercise that were too high? Be kind to yourself and start small. Perhaps just a 10 minute walk outside. You can always build it up slowly over time.

Try keeping a log of your exercise so that you can track your progress, share with your friends if you're happy to be open about it, or perhaps choose an accountability buddy and encourage each other to reach your goals.

For more inspiration here's a list of 50 different ways you can move your beautiful body without ever needing to step foot in a gym...

50 WAYS TO MOVE YOUR BODY
WITHOUT EVER NEEDING
TO STEP FOOT IN A GYM

1. Walking
2. Cycling
3. Yoga
4. Jogging
5. Intervals of running and walking
6. 10min abs workout (You Tube)
7. Swimming
8. Dancing
9. Tennis
10. Badminton
11. Squash
12. Hiking (including urban hiking)
13. Floor stretches
14. Wii Fit
15. Fitness ball workouts
16. You Tube videos
17. DVD workouts
18. Walking lunges
19. Stair climbing
20. Skipping
21. Trampolining
22. Jumping jacks
23. Buggy jogging
24. Netball

25. Roller Skating
26. Ice-skating
27. Climbing wall
28. Get a standing desk
29. Gardening
30. Park 10 mins away and walk
31. Geocaching
32. Get off the bus a stop early
33. Golf
34. Canoeing / Kayaking
35. Squats
36. Run around with your kids
37. Plank (holding yourself in a straight line balancing on your forearms and toes)
38. Walking your dog
39. Resistance bands
40. Tricep dips on a chair
41. Nike + Training Club (free app)
42. Take the stairs instead of the lift
43. Johnson & Johnson 7min Workout app
44. Wall sitting
45. Inchworm
46. Step ups on a bench or chair
47. DIY Dumbbells (water bottles)
48. Hoovering to pumping music
49. Press ups on your knees
50. Ahem... that thing couples do!

(Apps available at time of going to press)

HABIT #4: REAL LIFE STORIES

For yoga teacher Zaz (Zarouhi) Grumbar, moving her body daily became a practice that helped her mentally as well as physically and it's one that she continues to this day as a, role model for others;

"For years I felt that my body was a stranger to me, and more than that, as a teenager I felt slightly betrayed by being handed a size and shape that didn't tie in with what the 90s Kate Moss era seemed to expect (petite and curvy - early developer - versus willowy and androgenous). Cue an eating disorder that began in my mid-teens, and involved a fair bit of self-loathing and displacement of emotions. There was so much I was trying to avoid processing internally, and I projected it all onto my poor body.

Throughout that period, even in my early twenties when motherhood was a very very far off dream, I knew that I would only be able to be a parent if I resolved that part of me, exorcised some demons to make sure I wouldn't pass any of it onto my children. The irony was that eventually when I did get pregnant in my mid and late thirties, I absolutely adored my body and was in awe and admiration of the magic that it was doing!

But on the way to get there, there was of course, as we so commonly love to say in our modern times; "a journey". The biggest catalyst for change for me, and that I come back to every single day without fail was a two-fold practice. The first was discovering yoga, and more importantly, finding the style and teacher(s) that resonated with me. Static long holds, sitting down and stretching gently, focus on the external… no, not for me. Flowy, constant movements, focussed breath awareness, a moving meditation - oh yes! I fell in love with Vinyasa and Ashtanga, and my body no longer felt cumbersome or judged. Secondly, I was encouraged to be aware of my thoughts and of my own practice on my mat, but not be owned by it. My practice was not anyone else's, and it was thankfully, long before the arrival of wide scale social media."

Nila Mistry, a financial life planner and certified money coach who helps people feel confident and in control of their finances at Prosperity Life Planning has struggled with body confidence for years..

"Since my teens I've always been a little on the cuddly side. My parents worked for many years at Nabisco (previously National Biscuit Company) which meant we always had biscuits at home. You can imagine what my comforts were!

My weight yo-yoed until my late 20s. I felt frustrated, heavy, uncomfortable, and very unhappy. On reflection, I can see how this impacted my life, especially my personal relationships. I realise this was down to my own insecurities. That awareness made me think that something needed to change, I needed to take responsibility for the way I felt. I remember the energy quite clearly, a real determination to want to make a change. This feeling is what motivated me into doing something about it."

Nila started exercising regularly, joined a slimming club for support and began to feel good about herself again.

"I dropped a couple of dress sizes, felt amazing, grew in confidence and ended a toxic relationship. Three years later I met my husband, and we now have 2 beautiful children. I maintained that health regime for at least five years after I met my husband."

One of the key tennants of any habit is consistency but when Nila suffered five miscarriages as she and her husband tried to grow their family, her weight started to fluctuate, emotions took their toll and she struggled to maintain her routine. The impact hit her personal and business life.

"The impact on my business was that I found it easy to hide and beaver away behind the scenes just working on a 1:1 basis with my clients. As a financial planner it's important for prospective clients to know how I can help them create a sound financial future. But I found it challenging to market my services and wasn't showing my full potential and the value I delivered.

During lockdown in 2020 I turned 50 and that was the last straw. I felt fat and disappointed in myself that I still hadn't got to a place where I felt comfortable and loved the way I look. Personally, I had fallen out of love with myself and didn't feel like I was enough."

Nila realised that she needed to re-establish her routine and worked to find a new plan that suited her lifestyle and needs.

"It had accountability, support of a live online group with coaches and participants, a step-by-step guide of how to prepare and plan. I loved the idea of a structure, something to help me take that responsibility. The beauty of this was that I rediscovered my love for exercise again. Everything was planned and diarised. I started to feel stronger and more confident each day. I've now dropped a total of nearly three dress sizes since last May.

The habit strategy ideas I found in chapter 11 were really helpful, gettng into my gym clothes as soon as I brushed my teeth in the morning would be my cue to take 20mins get my abs and daily exercises complete. I recorded my workouts, and this meant I uploaded them to the group immediately after the workout. I set reminder alarms twice a week as they were the minimum workouts I needed to do. Batch cooking at weekends were a gamechanger. It meant I could eat on plan and on time."

Sometimes focusing on one habit can be the key to unlock others and as moving her body became part of Nila's regular routine again she began to see more than just a physical transformation.

"I noticed that I was able to look at myself more in the mirror, I was getting to know HER, the person I was avoiding, hiding behind, thinking I wasn't enough. As simple as this action is, it was a BIG gamechanger for me. I started to feel good about the way I looked, and I gave myself the time, space, and attention I needed. I was falling in love with myself.

I grew in confidence, I started to find my voice, for a long time I felt my opinions and thoughts weren't important - I wasn't important. This wasn't true. It was just stories, stories I made up because of how I felt about me. As I became happier, my family could see my sparkle had returned. I was starting to dream again and think of life's possibilities.

Now health and happiness are at the forefront of what's important to me. My family are my biggest driver to feel this this way. I want to be around for them, active and healthy. To inspire them to take responsibility for what they want to have, do and be. It's not always easy. There are days when I don't feel like it… but tapping into my why always helps me find my way back to my plan.

Life feels good. Professionally, I feel so much more confident in my business. I'm starting to create more educational videos for my social media, saying yes to projects and holding small workshops. You see Its not all about me now. The more I feel comfortable in my own skin, I can deliver more value to others."

MAKE THIS HABIT WORK FOR YOU

- Moving your body every day doesn't need to take ages, make you feel silly or ache in all the wrong (or right) places. This isn't about training for a marathon, it's about making exercise, and honouring your health and fitness, a habit for life.

- Even 10minutes at the beginning will make such a difference to your mindset so make a commitment and schedule that time into your routine when it works best for you.

- Be a body-moving role model - don't underestimate the positive impact of your friends, colleagues, family and kids watching you exercise regularly - you're modelling the way for a healthy lifestyle.

- Keep a log of your daily movement moments in the space below or in your journal including how you feel before and after, and any changes you notice in your body and mood.

- Everybody's body is different and what's right for one person won't necessarily be right for another, so make sure you get the OK from your doctor first if you have any health issues or concerns that might affect your ability to exercise and always start with something gentle and build up slowly.

YOUR NOTES

"Hold fast to dreams for if dreams die life is a broken-winged bird that cannot fly."
Langston Hughes

CHAPTER EIGHT

MY FIFTH HAPPINESS HABIT
Finding your WHY & dreaming bigger dreams

In the introduction I spoke about the importance of prioritising you and filling your own 'cup' before you try to serve other people in your life. One of the ways we can fill our cup is by knowing that we're heading in the right direction - that the actions we take every day are leading us slowly but surely towards our dreams, our vision, our ideal life.

So what does that ideal life look like? It will be different for everyone. For me, it started with a picture in my mind, a picture of me enjoying my days, smiling, laughing, enjoying time with my daughter, my friends, my husband and feeling good about myself again.

I kept that picture in my mind, reminding myself that I was working towards it every day. Over time my dream expanded and evolved until now I make it a ritual to reflect on my vision every 90 days or so and set clear intentions for how I'll make that vision a reality.

One of the things I love most about my Happiness Habits Transformation is that it helped me to set that vision by prioritising what matters most in my life. And it continues to do that, every day.

So far we've added thought-awareness, inspiration, gratitude, and movement to our daily routine - all habits that can boost our self-worth and positivity. In this chapter, I'm going to share my fifth habit and one that I'm especially passionate about; CLARITY. Specifically for me this means getting really clear about what matters to YOU and prioritising that in your life through a clear vision, specific goals and a realistic plan of what you need to do.

When I was working in the City, before our two children were born, I was ALL about goal planning, prioritising and action plans. I lived and breathed them. There was nothing I liked better than to tick off the completed actions in my Day-Timer® at the end of the day and go home feeling a real sense of satisfaction.

But while I was suffering with depression I completely lost my way for a time. I felt out of control, that I didn't have any time in the day for myself, that I didn't have a compass guiding me. Part of finding the way back to me was realising that I needed to dream again, to have something to work towards.

Over time I realised that setting and working towards a clear vision for myself boosted my satisfaction, reinvigorated my self-confidence, and upped my overall happiness. Research seems to bear this out, and Carole Ann Rice, life coach, author and owner of The Pure Coaching Academy agrees:

"Clarity comes from knowing ourselves, what we want, what it might look like, how it might resonate or satisfy us. Without self-awareness, it's hard to see what we desire in the future. I had my own moment of clarity some years ago when I was a Samaritan and wanted to help people in crisis. Many years later, having been made redundant from a newspaper I worked on, I hired a coach to help me decide what to do next and I didn't have a clue. Then looking back I joined the dots and realised I had always been interested in personal development and getting answers in life and helping others was what I loved most. The picture cleared and I got my focus at last!"

So let me ask you a question: Do you know where you want to be in six months' time? What about in one year, two years, five years?

Stephen Covey, author of "The 7 habits of highly successful people" calls this clear vision 'living with the end in mind'. Michael Hyatt calls it 'living intentionally'.

But essentially what they're both saying is that without a vision, without goals, without a plan, it's hard to live with purpose on purpose, and it's easy to get into a pattern of just drifting along, letting life control us rather than taking control of our lives.

Do you know where you're heading?
Do you have a vision mapped
out for your future?

Don't worry if you don't. Because in this chapter we're going to work through a series of exercises that will help you to dream your biggest dreams & recognise your purpose, break your dreams down into achievable goals, turn those goals into concrete actions and create a realistic plan using a simple four-step funnel to focus on what matters most to YOU.

THE FABULOUS 4-STEP FUNNEL TO FOCUSING ON WHAT MATTERS MOST

I like to have something visual to guide me when I'm working on my vision and goals and I find this four-step funnel so helpful. We're going to start at the top and work down the funnel, using each step to help give you a clear plan that you can start working towards straight away.

STEP ONE: DREAM IT

Have you ever felt like you're drifting along with the current of life, reacting to the twists and bends along the way but not really steering in one conscious and focused direction? Just like a boat on the river we need to set a course, but before we can do that we need to know where we're trying to get to.

So let's get our map and compass out shall we?

Exercise #1 - what really matters to you?

I want you to take a moment to think about something most of us try NOT to think about... your own mortality.

I hear you, we're starting off thinking about death? Look, the only real certainty in life is that one day we won't be here anymore. But our legacy will be. So let's put our imaginations to work for a moment or two...

In this exercise, I want you to think about what you would like the most important people in YOUR world to say about you at your funeral. Yup, it's a bit morbid I know, but look this is really what everything comes down to.... what you leave behind for others. Write the answers to these questions below or in your journal:

I WANT MY FAMILY TO SAY…

I WANT MY FRIENDS TO SAY...

I WANT MY COLLEAGUES/ CO-WORKERS TO SAY...

When I first did this exercise it stopped me in my tracks. I realised that, amongst other things, I wanted to create a lasting legacy not with wealth but with transformation. I realised that my true purpose was to share what

I've learned to help others and ultimately that led me to retraining and starting my coaching business.

What has this exercise taught you about YOUR purpose?

Exercise #2 - what are you passionate about?

Now I want you to think about the things that make you come alive! What makes your heart sing, your pulse race, your smile widen? What did you love doing as a child/teen? What do you wish you had more time for? What aspects of your job or business would you do even if you weren't paid to? Make a list of these things below or in your journal.

Exercise #3 - dreaming big dreams

This is where you get to dream BIG! Based on your purpose from exercise #1 and your passions from exercise #2, we're going to create a vision for your future based on four areas of your life - home/family/relationships, work/business, finances, and YOU.

Of course, the broader your vision the vaguer it can seem, so I'm going to challenge you to be as specific as possible here. Try to visualise your dreams as exactly where you want to be, how you want to feel, what you want to achieve, who you want to impact and how.

I call these Biscuit Dreams because our biggest and most exciting dreams can be so sweet and tempting!

But it's also a reminder that each dream should have certain qualities to make them come alive:

B	BIG	We're talking huge, audacious dreams here!
I	INSPIRING	Will this dream make you jump out of bed in the morning?
S	SCARY	Is it going to take you outside your comfort zone and send a delicious shiver down your spine?
C	COULD, NOT SHOULD	Suspend your inner perfectionist and be authentically you
U	UNWAVERING	Does this dream nag at the corners of your mind?
I	INTENTIONAL	Is it within the sphere of your control & specific to you?
T	TERRIFIC	Does it make you grin from ear to ear? Great!

Take some time to sit quietly and visualise your dreams as reality - use your senses to see, hear and feel them in your body. Write down each dream in your journal or using the space below with as much detail as possible relating to these four areas of your life - you, your home/family/relationships, your work/business and your finances.

Here's some questions to help you - in your dreams....

- What is your lifestyle like?
- What has changed in your life? What have you started doing/restarted/let go of?
- How do you feel about your friendships/relationships?
- Where are you living?
- What is on the desk in front of you?
- What kind of work are you doing?
- What part does money/financial stability play in your dreams?
- How do you feel about yourself?
- How is your health, your fitness?
- What does your day look like?
- Who are you working with/spending quality time with?
- How do you feel at the end of the day?

So tell me, how do you feel about your Biscuit Dreams? Are they big and a little bit scary? That's great. Just imagine how amazing you'll feel when you start to realise them...

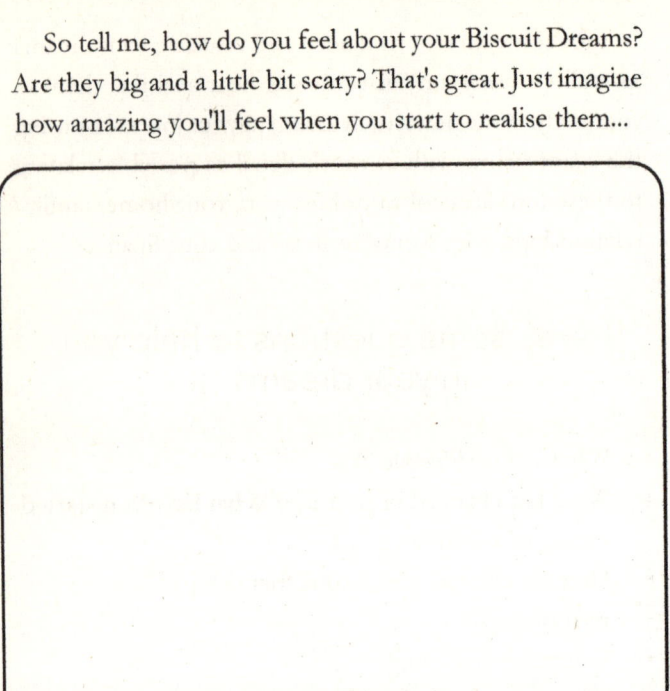

STEP TWO: PLAN IT - TURNING YOUR DREAMS INTO GOALS

Having goals helps to give our lives purpose and meaning, gives us a real sense of achievement when we reach them, and boosts our confidence that we can set out to do something and actually complete it.[17] Even stumbling along the way and picking ourselves back up to keep going has positive effects, building our resilience and helping us to cope with setbacks.

So now we're going to turn your Biscuit Dreams into exciting, measurable and manageable goals that you can work towards. You've probably heard of the acronym S.M.A.R.T to help you create goals but I like to call these S.M.I.L.E goals instead because just the thought of achieving them should make you grin. (Each letter is still a reminder of the qualities our goals should have so feel free to use whichever system you prefer.)

S	SUCCESS DRIVEN	Is there a specific successful result in your goal?
M	MEASURABLE	How will you know when you reach your goal?
I	INDIVIDUAL	Is your goal specific to you and under your control?
L	LONG, MEDIUM & SHORT TERM	Does this goal fit into your long & medium term ambitions with a plan from NOW to success?
E	EXCITING	Does it send a tingle down your spine and make you want to get started right away?

Here's an example of a SMILE goal written in a very specific way...

"I will finish reading The Happiness Habits Transformation and try out each habit in my daily routine by 31 January which will feel amazing because I will have a simple daily routine that will allow me to prioritise ME and MY happiness every single day."

This is a SMILE goal because it's success driven; I know specifically what I'm going to do, it's achievable because I have everything I need, it's relevant because it fits my longer term goal to find space in the day for me and be happier every day and I have a deadline for completing it. You'll also see that there's an extra part to the goal... the WHY. When we add our 'why' into a goal it makes it so much easier to stay motivated.

But let me just say here that for me, one of the most important parts of SMILE goals is that they are under your control and achievable. Because without that, we can't have balance in our lives. Striving for unattainable goals (whether that's being happy ALL the time or losing 10lb in 2 days) is a short-cut to being discouraged! But listen, you can also do more than you think you can my friend, so don't skimp on the self-belief.

Just make sure that there are enough hours in the day for you to do what you need to without compromising on self-care, like sleep and healthy eating, and on the important people in your life.

To start creating your SMILE Goals we're going to take each of the Biscuit Dreams you envisioned in Step One and brainstorm what you could do to bring those dreams to life. Then we're going to create specific Smile Goals that will help you to take the first steps to making your vision a reality.

Start by writing out the dreams that you want to work on below or in your journal:

MY BISCUIT DREAMS:

Now I want you to think about your current situation. How far are you away from those Biscuit Dreams? What do you have/not have in place to help you create your dreams? What do you need? What barriers or obstacles might get in your way? How could you overcome them? Who could you ask for help or guidance?

Make some notes here or in your journal:

WHAT COULD I DO?

This is the fun bit! Now you're going to brainstorm all the things that you could do to help you create your beautiful vision and live those dreams. And when you're brainstorming don't hold back! Write down everything that comes to mind below or in your journal, even if it feels too big or too crazy. Don't judge each idea at this stage, we just want to capture all thoughts at the moment.

OK, let's be real... there are only so many hours in the day right? So we need to take all those *coulds* that you just brainstormed and filter out the ones that are just not going to be realistic for you right now. And this is really important because as I mentioned earlier, having realistic goals means you're more likely to stay on track and start feeling a sense of achievement right away.

To get started you're going to take each of your coulds and separate them into three categories:

1. These coulds feel most rewarding/challenging/ thrilling for me

2. These coulds feel most realistic/quickest/ easiest for me

3. These coulds don't feel like a good fit for me right now

It's time to make some decisions

Now we're going to take the coulds from the first two categories above and turn those into Smile Goals. (You can keep the ones in the last category on the back burner for now but don't throw them out! You might want to come back to them if your circumstances change.)

Use the Smile checklist above to make sure each goal is success driven, measurable, individual, long-medium-short term, and super exciting! Then write out each goal below or in your journal using this format:

I will [insert your specific result written as a success] by [insert date] which will be amazing because [insert the impact on you / your customers / your family etc].

STEP THREE: DO IT - CREATING A REALISTIC ACTION PLAN

In steps one and two you envisioned your dreams and created clarifying goals to help you reach them. It's a magical thing to get your dreams and goals down on paper! But a goal without a plan is just a wish, and I'm passionate about you actually living those dreams.

So now we're going to work through Step #3: 'Do It!' and create a realistic action plan that will get you the results you're looking for.

Sometimes when we're learning something new it can be easier to see how someone else does things, can't it? So let me introduce you to Rachel. Rachel has two children aged 8 and 4 and we're going to create an action plan for one of her Biscuit Dreams to show just how it can be done.

Rachel's Biscuit Dream is to feel more confident and have more energy to play with her kids when they go on holiday. She's turned that into a Smile Goal like this:

"I will lose 10lbs and get fitter before our holiday in 90 days which will be amazing because it will boost my energy and confidence."

This is a Smile Goal because Rachel knows exactly what needs to get done and when she needs to get it done. It's measurable because she can see her weight loss on the scales and feel how much easier it is to play with her kids, and it's personal to her because she has ultimate control over her results.

It also fits with her longer-term dream to feel more confident and have more energy, and it's exciting because Rachel knows she's doing something for HER that will have a knock-on effect on the rest of her family.

So how does Rachel go about creating an action plan for that goal?

Let's break it down step by step...

Exercise #1: What do I need to do?

The first thing Rachel does is brainstorm all the tasks that she'll need to complete in order to reach her goal. To do this Rachel scribbles out all her ideas on a piece of paper making a note of her goal at the top of the page. She needs to consider the tasks, any research she needs to do, resources, training, and who she might need to get help from.

Some of the tasks on Rachel's brainstorm could include...

► Research the local gym and swimming pool, find out when they open, what facilities they have, and how much it costs to join. Download the Couch to 5K app on my phone.

- Speak to my friend Claire who is a nutritionist about how I could change my diet to lose weight, while keeping all the nutrients I need, and boosting my energy
- Speak to my family about my goal and get their support to help me be accountable - I can't do it all on my own!
- Create a vision board for our holiday with gorgeous pictures of our destination, clothes, and other ideas to keep me motivated for the next 3 months
- Ask my best friend Amanda if she will be my accountability buddy to help me stay on track with my goal (and remind her not to offer me that extra biscuit when I pop round for coffee!)
- Start walking the kids to and from school every day instead of driving to get some extra exercise.
- See if some of the school Mums would like to start a jogging club once a week.
- Drink a cup of hot water and lemon in the morning to help boost my digestion
- Weigh myself once a week and journal about how I feel in my body to measure how close I am to my goal

Ok, it's your turn. In your journal or the space below brainstorm all the tasks that you'll need to do for YOUR Smile Goals.

MY SMILE GOAL

BRAINSTORM: (Things to consider: tasks, research, training and who you'll need help from)

MY SMILE GOAL

BRAINSTORM: (Things to consider: tasks, research, training and who you'll need help from)

MY SMILE GOAL

BRAINSTORM: (Things to consider: tasks, research, training and who you'll need help from)

MY SMILE GOAL

BRAINSTORM: (Things to consider: tasks, research, training and who you'll need help from)

Exercise #2 - In what order do i need to do these tasks?

Next, Rachel needs to decide the order that each task needs to be done in. Some tasks can be done at the same time, while some will need to come before, or after, other tasks. To help work this out Rachel adds each task onto a TIMELINE, thinking about what needs to be done first, second, third etc. If tasks can be done at the same time she adds them all to the same point on the timeline.

Over to you: use the timeline below to work out the order your tasks need to be done in. Or if you prefer, draw a timeline in your journal or on a plain piece of paper. Why not get creative? Use colours, photos, drawings, or whatever you like to make your timeline work for you.

START

GOAL COMPLETE!

Exercise #3 - What does this look like each month and each week of this month?

Rachel now has a timeline showing the order of all her tasks. She grabs her planner and writes each action next to the month it needs to be done in. Next she splits that down further to give herself a weekly action plan for the current month.

Why not further out? Well, you can of course plan out each week for the next six months if you want to but in my experience life doesn't always go to plan. Some tasks might take longer than we think, some take less time. So I prefer to map out the detail only one or perhaps two months ahead and review where I am each month to give me some flexibility to pivot if I need to.

It's your turn! In your planner highlight the monthly and weekly actions you need to take for each of your goals. Remember to take account of any other tasks or commitments you have so that you don't become overwhelmed.

Great! You now have a set of monthly and weekly tasks to help you achieve your amazing dreams. We're on the home stretch now... the final prioritising step is... (can you guess?) creating daily actions that will help you meet your weekly goals.

Rachel looks at all the actions she has for week one of her plan and writes them in her planner with realistic amounts of time for getting them done. She sees that Monday morning is out as she has a meeting with her accountant so she moves one of the tasks to the following week.

Ok, it's your turn. Let's look at next week and call that the 1st week of your new plan. What other commitments do you already have for that week? (Consider everything from business meetings to doctors appointments and special time with your children, partner or friends.) What time do you have left? That is your *available* time. Schedule your goal-related actions for the week into that available time. But I want you to pick no more than three actions per day.

Why just three?

I've found that it's all too easy to set yourself up for failure by putting too much on your to-do list. Having 1-3 actions feels achievable, so you're more likely to get started and less likely to let life distract you or become overwhelmed by how much you have to do.

Once those actions are complete you can go ahead and add another task from your weekly goals list (you'll know from your planning what's the most profitable next one to do,) or just take the extra time you have to do something you love, safe in the knowledge that you've achieved your key actions for the day.

STEP FOUR: REVIEW

Over the past three steps you've created your monthly, weekly and daily action plan - now the final step in this 4-step system is *review*.

In order for us to hit our goals and complete our actions we need to be focused, for sure. But reviewing is all about relaxing that focus for a moment and getting some altitude. Think of it as zooming up into the clouds and looking down on yourself; your goals; your plans; and your tasks.

Pausing to review and reflect each week, month, and quarter, means you can check that (using our river analogy again) your boat is still on course and heading in the right direction. By doing this you can make any changes necessary to keep yourself on track. You might need to change, add, or remove an action. You might need to ask for help from a friend or colleague. Or you might need to extend a deadline or split an action into smaller tasks depending on what has happened the previous week or month.

It's important that we keep this fluidity, so that we can react to the twists and turns that our 'river' will inevitably take!

When I'm reviewing my goals and plans, I use a simple set of questions each week, month and quarter to help me see how I'm shaping up: feel free to use these when you're reviewing your own goals:

WEEKLY REVIEW QUESTIONS:

- What have I achieved this week?
- What do I need to do more of?
- What is holding me back?

MONTHLY REVIEW QUESTIONS:

- What goals have I completed this month?
- Thinking about my Smile Goals, what would I LOVE to create next month?
- What have I noticed about myself / my life this month?
- What do I want to start or stop doing next month as a result of that awareness?

QUARTERLY REVIEW QUESTIONS:

- What goals have I completed this quarter?
- Thinking about my Biscuit Dreams, what do I need to prioritise next quarter?
- What have I learned about myself / my life this quarter?
- What do I want to start or stop doing next quarter as a result of that awareness?

Some thoughts on what to do when things don't go to plan...

It's inevitable. At some time or other, your plans are going to get derailed. That's life!

Whether something out of your control stops you in your tracks or you find yourself struggling with a mental obstacle to overcome, you need a toolkit that you can dip into when things don't go as planned so that you can get back on track sooner rather than later.

Here's are some suggestions for things to add to your 'toolkit':

► Use your weekly review to look back over your achievements from last week and realise how far you've come.

► Take a break - all work and no play make anyone dull, not just Jack! Schedule in some down time (and yes I do mean schedule it) and have some fun doing whatever makes you happy.

► Ring a friend and ask them what they appreciate most about you. Soak up that positivity! Or why not try Julie's 'Look at Me!' book from Chapter Ten to capture all the positive things that other people say about you?

► Get silent. Sit with the discomfort of getting off track. See what emotions it brings. Then let them go, knowing that this is just a moment in time that will pass.

► Get some fresh air - getting outdoors to a local park, wood or just in nature not only gives you a change of scene, it also lets your mind switch gear. Let your brain take a back seat while your body takes control. I find I'm at my most creative when I'm walking or working out - essentially when I'm not TRYING to be creative. Plus the injection of fresh air will boost your energy and give your positivity a lift. It's hard to feel down when you're drinking in the sights and sounds of nature.

▶ Top tip: practice mindfulness while you're out and about to make the most of the experience. Use all your senses and really live in the moment - what can you see, feel, hear, smell? If a negative thought arises, don't try to stop it, recognise it and then let it go and refocus on your senses again.

HABIT #5 - REAL LIFE STORY

Lucy Hutchinson is co-owner of Any Little Thing Ltd; a home help service for the elderly, an author, podcast presenter of The Ultimate Mums Club and Mum to four year old Sebastian.

I first met Lucy when she got in touch needing help with organising and growing her business. To say she fit a lot into her days was an understatement.

"Before meeting Michelle and reading The Happiness Habits Transformation I always felt physically and mentally drained. I felt like a little lost puppy some days, creating list after list after list with the continuous feeling of never reaching goals or achieving anything. Don't get me wrong, sometimes by fluke or sheer luck, days would turn out very well, however what I will say is it just didn't feel so organised. It felt like more of a battle to reach my goals. I'm lucky enough to have a fab business partner and we work amazingly together, but we agreed that if we didn't take action we'd just continue to plod along as we were, feeling stressed and disorganised when things didn't go according to plan."

When we reviewed their existing planning processes it was clear that the lack of structure was holding them, and their business, back. "The impact this had on my life and our business was quite difficult to admit to, but it was extremely apparent. Without claiming our goals as our own, we were forever wondering and without planning we were forever stuck in neutral."

Once she began implementing the four-step goal setting funnel, and in particular creating a realistic action plan, Lucy realised it had wider implications than just for her business.

"As well as following the other steps in The Happiness Habits Transformation, it has been very helpful to consistently work on and review the goal-setting habit, both in my business and in other areas of my life too. I choose my end goal, break that end goal down and work backwards until I get to where I am in the present day.

Without planning and goal setting I would not have taken the leap and launched my podcast.

Without planning and goal setting my mental health would have suffered a lot more through the pandemic.

Without planning and goal setting I wouldn't have done so much for and with my son and for our family.

Without planning and goal setting I wouldn't have set up

such a fantastic support group for mums. The idea wouldn't have even come to me I don't think.

Basically, without planning and goal setting, I wouldn't have been able to celebrate so many wins - which, by the way, is extremely important too. You must celebrate your wins! Life at work and at home would look more chaotic and I think, perhaps, I wouldn't be so excited for the future.

I do have to remind myself all the time how important it is to maintain this habit and sometimes I get dragged back into my old ways, however I quickly correct myself and get straight back to it. Sometimes, days don't always go as planned and sometimes they work out for the better, but I just feel so much clearer minded and so amazing for being far more organised."

MAKE THIS HABIT WORK FOR YOU...

- Go back over this chapter as many times as you need to create your Biscuit Dreams, Smile Goals and a realistic action plan to help you prioritise what really matters to you.
- Cement your dreams in your mind by getting creative and making a vision board to bring them to life. Using a piece of A4 or A3 card or paper, cut out pictures and images from magazines, and add words and colours to represent elements of your vision. Place it somewhere where you'll see it every day.
- Try to carve out 10 minutes each evening to review your weekly goals and set your priority actions for the next day. I do this every day, and it is so releasing to go to bed knowing that in the morning, I have a clear plan that is working towards my dreams.
- Each week, month and quarter, set aside time to review how you're doing, making course corrections if you need to, to stay on track.
- Remember that it's important not to beat yourself up when things don't go to plan and dip into your 'toolkit' if you need to.

"While it may seem small, the ripple effects of small things is extraordinary"
Matt Bevin

CHAPTER NINE

MY SIXTH AND SEVENTH HAPPINESS HABITS

Two terrific tools to boost your positivity in minutes

Tool #1: Get Cheesy For That Feel Good Glow

Will you do something for me? It sounds like a strange request but I want you to grab a pen or pencil and hold it between your teeth while you read the next few paragraphs. Go on, I'll wait while you do it. Don't worry there are no hidden cameras and the reason will become clear in a moment.

Ok, great. So now let me ask you a question; how often do you smile in, say, a day?

We all smile, right? We smile 100's of times a day. We smile because we're happy.

But hang on, there's a good chance that not all of these statements are true. We DO all smile, from time to time, and in fact smiling is a universal facial expression[18], but most of us adults actually smile less than we might think we do.

In the depths of my depression I found it hard to smile at all. Just the sheer physicality of moving the corners of my mouth felt exhausting. These days I try to remember to smile as often as possible. How about you? How often would you say you smile? If you're anything like the average adult you'll probably smile around 11 times a day.[19]

Doesn't seem a lot really, does it? And that's a shame because the simple act of smiling has SO many positive benefits for our health and mental wellbeing, from improving our overall mood and lowering our heart rate to reducing stress reactions and even predicting how long we'll live![20]

And after all there are a whole variety of things that can make us smile. A study by footwear brand Moshulu found the top ten things that UK participants smiled most about included sunshine, getting a compliment from a stranger, looking back at old photographs, hearing a baby laugh or seeing them smile, and having a hug.[19]

Dr. Jessamy Hibberd, a Chartered Clinical Psychologist involved with the study believes that even though smiling is a subconscious response to something we see, hear or feel, we should be considering it as an important part of our day.

But what if you don't feel like smiling? Surely we only smile because something makes us happy? Well, actually, it turns out we can also make ourselves happy by smiling.

When we feel happy, our brains produce endorphins and send signals to our facial muscles (specifically the zygomaticus major muscle around our mouth and the orbicularis oculi muscle around our eyes) to trigger a smile. But because our body and mind are inextricably linked, that physical act of smiling also tells our brain that we're happy, and causes a positive feedback loop.

And it's that feedback loop that we can harness to actually make ourselves feel happier.

Remember I asked you to hold a pen in your teeth earlier? (You can stop doing it now by the way!) I asked you to do that because holding a pen in that position mimics smiling.

We created the condition that I described above i.e. smiling without specifically being happy. And you might just find that you're in a more positive mood now than you were before you started reading this chapter. This is because our facial movements can influence our emotional experience and how we interpret life around us.

A really broad smile – and by that I mean a smile that turns up the corners of your mouth, pinches out your cheeks and wrinkles your eyes, known as the Duchennee smile and named after the French neurologist Duchenne de Boulogne – fires that signal to our brains. It stimulates our reward system to release those same endorphins; those lovely happy hormones I mentioned before.

Interestingly, it was Charles Darwin, more famous for his theory of evolution, who first suggested that our facial expressions, like smiling, can produce a parallel effect on our feelings.[21] And more recently in 2012, researchers Tara Kraft and Sarah Pressman found that it didn't actually matter if that smile was real or faked, the result was very similar. In fact, people in their study who smiled, either because they were asked to or because they held something in their mouths as you just did, felt more content, had lower heart rates and reduced stressed responses.[22] So smiling makes it easier to stay positive in stressful situations - something to remember the next time you're in a traffic jam and late for work!

But for now, let's do it again. A big, real smile. Go on, do it now. No, not a little smile, a big LIKE-YOU-MEAN-IT grin. And hold it for 10 seconds or so.

How do you feel? Did you experience a little burst of feel-good endorphins? Hopefully you felt a little bit happier as a result.

And this is why consciously SMILING regularly throughout the day (even if I don't really feel like it) is my sixth daily Happiness Habit. Do I feel a bit strange grinning on my own in my office? Sometimes! But the results are worth it.

Tool #2: Positive Perspective With Three Little Words

When my daughter Amelia was still very young she taught me a major lesson about how easy it could be to challenge my habitual negativity.

I've mentioned before about how I was a defensive pessimist for the longest time.

No, it's not sexy or cool like optimism, but for years it was my shield. I expected the worst and hoped for just ok. I scared myself witless thinking about all the bad things that could happen. My pessimism felt like a protective blanket, cushioning me from pain. If things weren't as bad as I thought they were going to be then I was pleasantly surprised. But if they were... well then I wasn't shocked.

Whether it was something as simple as the weather or as complex as a business strategy I was ready for everything to go wrong. I mean, I really had it down. If I was planning an event I'd expect it to rain so that no-one would come. If I tried a new idea at work I expected it to fall flat.

Documented by Dr Julie K Norem, Defensive Pessimism[23] is a strategy that people use to manage anxiety and work more productively. As Defensive Pessimists, we lower our expectations to help prepare ourselves for the worst. Then, we mentally play through all the bad things that might happen. Often in lots and lots of detail! This helps us to focus away from our emotions so that we can plan and act effectively.

Now, in some situations defensive pessimism can actually be helpful. It can, for example, help us to work out all the things that might go wrong at say, a conference we're planning, and make sure that we have strategies in place to deal with them. That seems only sensible, right?

But defensive pessimism is unhelpful when it makes us so fearful that we pull the brakes on something before we even get started. When that happens it's the opposite of a positive mental attitude helping to motivate us to do our best - we're actually failing ahead of time.

And yep, that was me exactly. Failing in my mind. And that negativity started to seep into my everyday language without me even realising it.

"We're going to be late for school again because you've been watching TV with your breakfast."

"I forgot to do the grocery order last night and now we're going to have to go to the shops."

"Eurgh it's raining and now the traffic is going to be terrible."

But then, one day, when I was standing in the kitchen with Amelia, I noticed an amazing thing. Whenever I said something negative as part of our everyday chit-chat, she had an automatic reaction to it. She simply said three little words that turned my negativity on its head.

"But at least..."

And abra cadabra my brain processed her positive message and I felt better.

"We're going to be late for school again because you've been watching TV with your breakfast."
"But at least you got to finish your coffee, Mummy."

"I forgot to do the grocery order last night and now we have to go to the shops."
"But at least we get to go together and buy something different, Mummy."

"Eurgh it's raining and now the traffic is going to be terrible."
"But at least we get to listen to the songs on the radio a bit longer, Mummy."

It was like magic. I don't know exactly why this works but it seems that my brain focuses on the last statement (hers) rather than the first (mine). The positivity of her statement tamed the negativity of mine.

And so I started using this technique myself. Whenever I noticed I was having a negative thought or saying a negative thing out loud, I followed it up straight away with a positive about the situation. Any positive.

"I look awful in this dress… I knew I shouldn't have bought it in the first place."
"But at least now I know that style doesn't suit me and if I gift it to the local charity store someone else who it does suit will get to enjoy it."

"No-one is going to buy this course, I shouldn't have even started creating it."
"But at least I'm at an early stage in creating it. I can put plans in place to get some feedback from potential customers before I sell it, to learn what works and what doesn't."

Now I'm not saying that I'm completely recovered. I definitely still slip into negative mode from time to time (my husband is quick to let me know when I do) but over time I've definitely become less defensively pessimistic and more optimistic. I've lost the fear and replaced it with hope.

And that is why those three simple little words *"but at least"* are my seventh happiness habit.

HABITS #6 AND #7 -
REAL LIFE STORIES

Lucy Hutchinson has found habit #6 benefits her in a number of ways;

"One of the habits I absolutely love is such a simple one, I feel every single person in the world can achieve it. Smiling. A smile always makes me feel positive and it really makes me happy when I smile at others, especially if the smile is reciprocated. I often smile at strangers, particularly those that look a little stressed or troubled and you can occasionally see their mood lift immediately. When I smile, I feel more positive. If I am working, I feel more focused and ambitious and if I am having a bad day, it can help switch my mood."

Victoria Welton is an award-winning professional photographer, blogger and radio presenter who has integrated habit #7 in her own life and seen the onward impact on her family.

"Something that has really stuck with me since reading The Happiness Habits Transformation is the positivity I have managed to inject into our family. One of the things that I experience regularly, especially from my partner, are comments which tend to bring people down. I can particularly recall one Saturday during the summer 2020. I had recently read about habit number seven and the positive spin of the words 'but at least' had really stuck with me.

The first lockdown was starting to lift, and we had driven to West Bay for a family day out. During the car journey, there was a lot of negativities around how we were going to distance, whether others would be wearing masks and if we should buy ice cream. Each time I responded with a sentence which included the words 'at least'. I responded to each negative comment - 'At least we have each other'. 'At least we have our health'. 'At least the sun is shining'. 'At least we are near the sea'. Ross started to understand what I was doing as did my teenage daughter, Grace, and in turn they have started to use it too. I have found that this is such a gentle way to encourage everyone to consider whether what they are experiencing is really all that bad in the grand scheme of things. It makes it easy to softly make changes without any form of guilt."

MAKE THESE TWO
HABITS WORK FOR YOU

- Practise smiling regularly through the day, whether you feel like it or not, to give yourself a little mood 'boost'.

- To make it easier to remember, set an alarm on your phone, put a post-it note in the car, on your desk or wherever you'll see it regularly throughout the day, simply saying SMILE.

- Spread the joy! It's difficult not to smile back at someone when they're directly smiling at you, so share a positivity boost with someone else by cranking out a big cheesy grin, knowing that if they smile back you're helping them get all those lovely healthy benefits too.

- If you're already adding habit #1 into your day with some daily meditation, try adding a gentle smile to your lips at the beginning of your practice and see if it helps you to be kinder to yourself when your mind wanders.

- For a bit more of a chuckle (and a smile) take a look at Ron Gutman's fabulous and funny TED talk.[24]

- Try to recognise when you're thinking a negative thought or saying something negative and use the three little words "but at least..." followed by something positive.

- Notice how these two simple tools impact on your positivity when you add them to your daily routine and make a note of it below or in your journal.

MY NOTES

"Acknowledge all of your small victories.
They will eventually add up to something great."
Kara Goucher, American long distance runner

CHAPTER TEN
MY EIGHTH HAPPINESS HABITS
Your daily success party plan!

I strongly believe that a great morning follows a great evening. And in this chapter we're going to build on the habit we created in chapter six - practising gratitude - with a habit for the end of each day - celebrating success.

We all like to celebrate success in our lives, right? From family occasions like birthdays and kid's 'firsts' to our sports teams winning a game or a trophy. It feels great to throw our hands up and yell hurray!

But it's so easy in the daily hustle and bustle to focus on what hasn't gone well in our day, and forget to see what actually has. So I want to show you how you can bring a little bit of that positive energy into your every day, and go to bed feeling fulfilled and ready for tomorrow, by celebrating the small things that happen in our lives.

One of the mood-boosting techniques that I learned in my therapy sessions was writing down three to five things that had gone well in my day. At the time creating my 'happy list' was easier said than done and I really struggled in the beginning to find three things. But interestingly, by consciously looking for something, *anything*, positive in my day, things started to slowly but surely show up.

And it didn't matter if those things were minor improvements over the previous day, the sun popping out on a rainy morning or my daughter settling herself for a nap without me holding her hand the whole time. Just that act of recognising that I could see the good in my day was enough to lift my mood.

Thurs 11 March 2010

1. Good therapy session.
2. Amelia fed outside of the apartment (if only briefly).
3. Bought a new sling.
4. Had a half hour playdate.
5. Amelia settled herself to sleep at 4pm for an hour.

When I was building my Happiness Habits routine I wanted to take that recognition of the positives one step further and turn it into a celebration of my achievements - however big or small - because I knew from experience how ending the day this way was a great way to boost my mood and stay motivated.

Remember in chapter eight I talked about building resilience for those inevitable times when you get off track with your goals and priority actions? I suggested looking back over your achievements and using those other wins to boost your confidence and give you a lift. Your daily success list is where you're going to regularly and intentionally celebrate and record those achievements.

And I'm not alone in doing this. In the workplace, big businesses are realising the importance of celebrating small wins with their employees as a way to create a more productive and positive working environment. The Harvard Business Review found that even the smallest step forward has a big impact on employee satisfaction. This 'progress principle' was even more powerful and made employees happier in their job when they felt they were moving forward with 'meaningful' work.[25]

So whether you're working for someone else, yourself, or just want to get a little positivity boost, we're going to put this exact principle to work for us with my eighth and final habit.

We've already started working on your 'meaningful' work in chapter eight with your exciting dreams, goals and action plans. And now habit #8 adds in the important second part - the recognition of your progress, by celebrating the small wins in each and every day. Think of it like your personal success party plan!

3 REASONS TO CELEBRATE

Here's 3 great reasons to recognise and celebrate even the smallest wins in your day…

1. Attitude and motivation

When we celebrate a success we shift into a 'winning' mindset which is upbeat, optimistic and positive. By making these daily celebrations a habit we can end the day with confidence and self-belief. We're fired up for tomorrow, rather than letting negative thoughts about what could have gone better play over and over in our minds.

At the end of the day, what's past is past - don't dwell on it! Instead, we can celebrate each priority action begun or ticked off, each weekly goal established or achieved and boost our motivation to keep going by seeing the progress we're making.

2. Learning and building

When we recognise even the smallest successes we can start to try to understand why they worked, how they worked, what we did that made that happen and how we can repeat it across other actions, goals, and areas of our lives.

3. The happiness factor

In the last chapter I talked about how consciously smiling can release chemicals in our brains that make us feel happier. In a similar way, dopamine is released in our brains when we achieve something we set out to do. Dopamine is a neurotransmitter, often called the "feel good" neurotransmitter, which tells the brain that whatever it just experienced is worth focusing on and getting more of - it makes us feel great![26]

By building in a success habit every evening, we can prime ourselves to end the day with a beautiful dose of satisfaction. It's like a nightly supplement for your mindset.

HABIT #8: REAL LIFE STORY

Julie Brown celebrates her achievements with her 'Look at Me' book. This isn't about ego but celebrating the things that she's proud of and the things that make others feel happy.

"My most troublesome mindset monkey is imposter syndrome. I'm what some would call a 'high achiever' with years of success in some very stressful environments under my belt. And yet I'm hit with the wobbles and 'when will I be found out' thoughts on a regular basis. Or at least I used to be. My little book of goodness has helped me get this under control (mostly) and things are much more on an even keel now," she says.

Julie recognised how quick we all are to ignore the positive things we do, our accomplishments, however small they might seem. As she points out; "It's just that society, social media and a lifetime of too-much-telly blast out the message that to be a hero you have to wear a cape."

"I've had the opportunity to make real differences to others, raised a family, ridden motorbikes across continents, snowboarded down black runs, am planning to walk to Everest Base Camp, make my own clothes and can even change the clock on my oven without looking at the instructions. Yet even with all these achievements my mind was tricking me into thinking I'm not good enough. Every. Single. Day. The negative thoughts were turning up so often I eventually gave them a name – Betty."

And creating a 'Look at Me book' is really simple. Julie suggests finding a notebook that will fit in your back or pocket and making it your constant companion.

"Mine is a Christian Lacroix beauty that my son bought for me, which makes it extra special. As soon as you get it, start to write out all the things you've achieved, the things you're good at, things you've done that make you feel proud, and the lovely things other people have said or written about you.

Do this quickly – it's not something to ponder over for hours. Think about everything, no matter how small. You make a mean curry? Put it in there. Great feedback from your boss? Put it in there. You're happy with your hair. Put it in there. You are kind, you give to charity, you passed your driving test the first time, you recently learnt to swim. Put it all in there. Get to 100 points as quickly as you can. If you have emails with compliments on them, or testimonials, print them out and stick them in the book too. Fill it with lots of goodness.

And remember, this is your 'Look at Me' book for life. So, keep adding to it. Every day if you can."

Julie describes her 'Look at Me' book as a "positive umbrella to fight off the black clouds and emotional storms." But it only works if you USE it. If negativity surfaces she advises to grab your book and read a page or two to remind you how good you actually are.

"Don't let your brain fool you into thinking anything else. This book is proof that there is no need to feel anything but fantastic. Read it out loud if you need to give your brain the message in a more powerful way. That'll soon shut it up.

I look at mine every single morning to put myself in the right frame of mind for the day ahead. It helps me breeze through the tasks that would usually be battered by Betty. Because I carry it with me, I can also grab it as and when something troublesome comes along. I find it particularly useful if I know I'm going to be having a tricky conversation with someone and when dealing with difficult people. It's an amazing way to stay focused on you and your greatness."

MAKE THIS HABIT WORK FOR YOU

- Set aside a specific time every evening to think through your day and recognise what went well.
- Use your planner, a 'Look at Me' book like Julie's or the space below to note three (or more) successes each day.
- Remember - these can be anything from completing one of your daily priority actions to managing to get some time to yourself. Celebrating even the smallest of wins makes us feel like we're making progress - a great positivity boost!
- At the end of each week read over your daily successes and add them into your weekly goals review from chapter eight to give you the motivation to keep going. Look how much you've achieved! (You totally deserve a special treat as a reward for your progress.)
- Look back over each success and feel great about it. "Every day may not be good... but there's something good in every day" (Alice Morse Earle) So seek it out and celebrate it!

MY NOTES

"You'll never change your life until you change something you do daily. The secret of your success is found in your daily routine."
John C Maxwell

CHAPTER ELEVEN
BRINGING IT ALL TOGETHER
How do habits work anyway and how can you put them to work for YOU?

In the last ten chapters you've learned about the happiness habits that I use as the ingredients in my own personal recipe for boosting my positivity every. single. day.

But knowing the things we need to do to make us happier and actually DOING them are two very different things. After all, if we're honest we all know that eating junk food, drinking too much alcohol and not exercising regularly doesn't constitute a healthy lifestyle. In the past when I was working with a new coaching client, they often fully aware of what they needed to do to make a significant change in their lives, but for whatever reason (and there can be many) they weren't doing those things. The knowing just isn't enough.

Since 2009 I've learned a lot about the activities that boost my everyday contentment. Everything you've read so far in this book, in fact. But those things didn't make a strong, positive and long-lasting impact on my life, until they became *habits*. And it was the repetition of those habits in an easily achievable *routine* that really made a huge difference for me.

When I realised this I became fascinated with habits - after all they'd helped me to become a happier me! So in this chapter I'll share with you what I've learned about how habits are formed, and how to create the best possible environment for your new habits to make sure they 'stick' and become a regular part of your day.

There's a lot of neuroscience behind some of our seemingly simplest habits, but rather than delving deep into synapses and neural pathways, what I hope to do here is give you some useful knowledge about how our brains have evolved to use habits and how you can harness that to make your own Happiness Habits Transformation work for you.

So as I mentioned earlier, we now know eight specific ways to create a growth mindset and boost your positivity, but the 'knowing' isn't enough. To make that knowledge really work for us, we can do two key things.

The first key thing is that we can use it. It's common parlance that knowledge is power but I agree with Dale Carnegie who said "Knowledge isn't power until it's applied." There are various ways to do this - you can apply it straight to your own life, today, and experience the outcomes for yourself. Or you can share it with someone else - The Feynman Technique (named after Nobel Prize winning physicist Richard Feynman) suggests that when you share knowledge, you get to experience it again for a second time. By breaking down complex ideas and explaining them to others, you embed it more strongly within your own mind. You could try explaining one of the chapters in this book in your own words to a friend or colleague for example.

The second key thing is that we can combine the knowledge with a 'habitual' behaviour - a habit - to make it a regular beneficial part of our daily lives. So how do we do that?

Well first, let me ask you a question - before you picked up and started reading this book, what was the very first thing you did this morning? I'm guessing that you might have brushed your teeth, jumped in the shower, made a cup of coffee or tea, or perhaps made your bed.

These activities feel like choices but studies have shown that more than 40% of the actions we perform every day are habits rather than conscious decisions.[27]

So it seems we're already very adept at creating habits in our daily lives, we just don't realise that we're doing it.

A habit is any regularly repeated behaviour that requires little or no thought and is learned rather than natural to us.[28] Our habits impact what we do, and how and when we do it.

Let's take brushing our teeth as an example. I brush my teeth when I get up in the morning and before I go to bed at night. I do this every day, I don't really have to think about when or where to do it and I don't consider 'how' to do it either. It just sort of happens.

Except that of course it doesn't just happen. In fact if we go back in time to when I was a child learning how to brush my teeth, I had to be told when and where to do it and had to think carefully about how to do it.

Whether we brush our bottom teeth first or our top ones, left or right side, spit or swallow the toothpaste, these are all learned behaviours. We learn a sequence of actions with a specific outcome that takes place in a particular way. And because they're reinforced by our parents, teachers, dentists, societal norms and even, to a certain extent, advertising, we repeat them day in, day out; they become habits.

And there's a very good reason for this - we've evolved this way to make our brains as efficient as possible.

In the same way that our computers and mobile phones perform routine tasks in the background while we check our emails, our brains don't want to waste valuable conscious effort repeating tasks that can be done by our unconscious mind without our input. If we had to consciously think about every action we perform, our brain would be overloaded with the simplest of tasks like walking and chewing.[29]

So our brains developed the ability to recognise the actions that we perform repeatedly and move them from conscious processing, where we have to think about them, to unconscious processing, where we don't. Clever!

How do we use this information to help us create our Happiness Habits as habits?

The key here is to understand how the habit functions as an action. In his fascinating book 'The Power of Habit' Charles Duhigg explains how researchers at MIT found three distinct parts to a habit that occur in order: a cue, a behaviour, and a reward. These three parts create a 'habit loop' and it's this that governs the habit taking place.[30]

Essentially, when a cue happens a behaviour is triggered and that is followed by a positive reward. The reward then acts as motivation the next time the cue takes place and so on.

So if we think about the habit of making a cup of coffee at the same time every morning; the cue is the time of day, the behaviour is making a cup of coffee, and the reward is that it tastes good and we get a hit of caffeine that wakes us up!

Habits are also formed when we become really good at doing something. Let's use that tooth brushing idea again. Think back to brushing your teeth this morning. The first time you learned how to do this as a child, you probably had to concentrate on every single action. From measuring out the right amount of toothpaste, to learning how to hold the brush, how hard or soft to press and how to spit out the foam instead of swallowing it , you will have focused all your attention on each and every step. And you were likely also keenly aware of how difficult it seemed. Whenever we learn something new we tend to recognise our limitations - we're what's known as *consciously unskilled*.[31]

After a while, we move through a process of development, learning, and practice so that we become better and better at all the steps. We still need to think about measuring and brushing but it doesn't feel quite so challenging. We're now *consciously skilled*.

Still more time passes and eventually we're brushing our teeth without even thinking about what we have to do or the order we have to do it in. We're now *unconsciously skilled*.

We can easily think about other things while we're brushing away, like mentally planning our schedule for the day, because our brain has stored each step of the process in the order that it needs to be done. It's also become super efficient at doing all of those steps and can run automatically in the background. We have formed these steps as habits.

In reading this book and starting to practice the eight Happiness Habits you are going through a similar process. You're learning a series of new behaviours that might feel a bit strange right now. Fitting them into your day is an effort, you have to consciously schedule in time for them and some days you might forget altogether.

Each chapter has taught you a behaviour - thought awareness, inspiration, gratitude, movement, clarity, smiling, perspective and celebration - and, hopefully, you're starting to feel the reward as a positive feeling after you've done them.

Now we can start using the three parts of the habit loop to cement these behaviours as habits in your existing daily routine. We have the behaviours, the middle part of the loop, so let's look at the first part, the cue or reminder.

YOUR HAPPINESS HABITS REMINDERS

When you're trying to build new habits, you can create reminders for the behaviour that you want to make a habit. Those reminders can be anything you like but research has shown that ideally they should be an event or activity that is already established in your daily routine.[32] That's what will make the habit 'sticky'.

This is a really important part of the habit-forming process. I know that the reason so many other habits I tried to create didn't stick with me, is that I didn't align them with my already established routine. They stuck out a bit, felt awkward and uncomfortable or I just plum forgot about them. And so, after a while, I quit. So I'd definitely recommend making your reminders something you're already doing regularly and routinely.

These reminders could include:

- ▶ Your alarm going off at the same time every morning
- ▶ Brushing your teeth
- ▶ Making your bed
- ▶ Making a morning cup of tea or coffee or a smoothie
- ▶ Checking your mailbox
- ▶ Checking your phone
- ▶ Waiting for the train or bus on your commute
- ▶ Getting into the car on the way to work
- ▶ Getting out of the car when you get home
- ▶ Going to the same coffee shop or restaurant for lunch
- ▶ Sitting down at your desk to start work
- ▶ Tidying your desk at the end of the day
- ▶ Reading a book at bedtime

You can use these existing events or activities as reminders for the new habit that you want to create by placing the new habit either before or afterwards. For example, if you want to drink more water and you know that you routinely make five cups of coffee a day, you could use that as your cue to drink a glass of water while your coffee is brewing. Then go one step further and make it easier to remember by putting an empty glass by your coffee maker.

Here are some of the reminders that I use for my own Happiness Habits every day:

REMINDER	BEHAVIOUR
My alarm clock goes off	I get up and put on my gym kit so I'm all ready to exercise (Habit #4).
I've finished my morning exercise	I do a short meditation or journal **(Habit #1)**
I get to my desk where my planner page is open next to an inspiring book I placed there the night before.	I do my gratitude practice **(Habit #3)**, read an inspiring passage from the book **(Habit #2)** and use my planner to get clear on my priorities for the day based on my goals **(Habit #5)**.
I notice the 'Smile' sticky note on my coffee cup	I smile a big, broad smile and enjoy the mood boost! **(Habit #6)**
I notice that I've thought or said something negative	I say 'but at least...' and focus on one positive thing **(Habit #7)**.
I'm clearing my desk at the end of the day	I write down what went well today and celebrate those achievements **(Habit #8)**.

As you can see my reminders are spread throughout the day. Some are parts of my routine that were already established before I started my Happiness Habits (like my alarm clock going off and clearing my desk at the end of the day) and others I've consciously created - leaving my planner open on my desk at night, for example. But what they all have in common is that now they are already present in my daily life - I don't have to think about them - which makes it easier to use them as reminders or anchors for my Happiness Habits.

Essentially the pattern goes like this: When I do X, I will do Y or when I think about doing A I will do B first.

Which of these habits do you think is the hardest for me to maintain? For me it's habit #7 because it doesn't have a 'material' cue. Instead it relies on me recognising that I've thought or said something negative... but over time I've become better and better at that. Plus I get a lot of help from my kids and my husband too!

But this also leads me to the important final ingredient in the habit recipe - perseverance. Even when your new habits are 'stuck' to an existing routine activity, it's going to take time for you to become unconsciously skilled at them.

And please don't worry if you miss a habit one day - as well as showing that it's important to repeat behaviours to make them habits, studies have also shown that missing an opportunity to perform a behaviour does not materially affect the habit formation process.[33]

OK, it's your turn. Think about the reminders that you could use in the morning, during the day and in the evening for your new Happiness Habits. Make a note of them below or in your journal:

The cues I will
use in the morning:

The cues I will
use during the day:

The cues I will
use in the evening:

YOUR HAPPINESS HABITS REWARDS

If you've started practising some of the Happiness Habits you could already be feeling a positivity boost. But you might also find some of the habits more challenging than others. It took me a long time to be comfortable sitting with my thoughts in my meditation practice, for example. I felt frustrated and impatient and that completely removed the 'reward' I was meant to be feeling!

Please believe me when I say that over time my practice has definitely created the reward I was looking for, but in this situation, you can also give yourself a *stand-in reward* to help complete the habit loop until it feels more natural.

If you have children you're probably familiar with stand-in rewards - they form the basis of reward charts for positive behaviour and to instil habits like regular tooth brushing or putting away toys.

Here are some stand-in rewards you could consider:

- ▶ Having a cup of coffee/tea when you've finished your gratitude practice
- ▶ Putting money in a jar every time you complete a thought awareness session and buying something for yourself after 20 sessions
- ▶ Not picking up your phone or allowing yourself to visit a social media site until you've done your daily priority planning.
- ▶ Buying yourself some new workout clothes or a new swimsuit when you've moved your body every day for 2 weeks.

Over to you! Think about the rewards that will be most motivating for you and make a note of your ideas here or in your journal...

The rewards that will motivate me:

How I could use them
to reward my Happiness Habits:

And finally, here's how I weave each of the eight Happiness Habits into my daily schedule:

- ▶ My alarm goes off and I put on my gym kit so I'm all ready to exercise (habit #4) followed by a short meditation or journaling (habit #1)

- ▶ When I'm at my desk with a cup of coffee I read something inspiring (habit #2) and then write down 3 things I'm grateful for (habit #3).

- ▶ Then I look at my weekly goals and three priority actions for the day (habit #5) and check that they're still the most important actions I can take. (At the weekend I review my week and plan for the following week, writing out my new weekly goals.)

- ▶ During the day I'll work on my three priority actions, practice smiling and saying 'but at least' whenever I think a negative thought or hear myself saying one - that is if my daughter doesn't get there first! (Habits #6 & #7)

- ▶ In the evening, while I'm clearing my desk, I write down my successes from the day (habit #8), tick off any of my completed tasks from my weekly goals sheet and make a note of the next day's three priority actions. I can set my alarm at night feeling satisfied that I've achieved something that day and knowing what I'm going to be focussing on tomorrow.

MAKE THIS WORK FOR YOU:

- Create reminders for each of the Happiness Habits that you want to build into your daily routine. Make your habits more 'sticky' by choosing reminders that are already part of your regular routine.

- You can support your reminders by preparing the things you need for a particular habit i.e. putting your gym kit by the bed the night before for habit #4.

- If you're finding some of the habits more challenging than others, create some stand-in rewards that you can use to support your habit 'loop'. Over time, once the result of the habit itself is rewarding, you can drop the substitute reward (or keep it if it makes you happy!)

- Remember that it can take quite a while to establish new habits so be patient with yourself and don't be put off if you forget to perform one of the habits occasionally.

"Change is inevitable. Growth is optional."
John C. Maxwell

CHAPTER TWELVE
UP TO DATE WITH A BANG
How my Happiness Habits are
supporting me through perimenopause

It's been three years since this book was first published, and as I sit here typing this, I'm waiting for a call from my GP. We're going to discuss changing the dose of my hormone replacement therapy or HRT.

But let me back it up a bit.

Relishing the euphoria of my first published book, I had no idea that three years later a bucket load of things would hit me simultaneously - the Covid-19 pandemic, homeschooling two children while working two businesses, reeling from my Mother's stroke and other behind-the-scenes family matters... and becoming perimenopausal.

Fast forward to Jan 2021 and England had entered its third national lockdown. Suddenly I was right back there again, in the weeds of my mind as I had been years before, dealing with too much in one go and not knowing quite how I was going to cope with it all.

At the time I was the director of a US personal development company alongside running my own coaching business. I remember sitting at the dining room table, one child next to me filling out a maths worksheet, the other in the playroom having an online science lesson, while I was planning for my next coaching client and waiting for a Zoom meeting to start with my colleagues in the US..

Like most days during this time, my stress level started the day at def con two and stayed there once I'd tucked the kids in for sleep and gone back to work at my desk for another couple of hours. When I finally fell into bed in the early hours of the following day, I was mentally exhausted and brain dead.

And then the brain fog and hot flushes began.

I put the new symptoms down to stress even after having fluctuating hormones for over a year. I knew stress could affect a string of brain and body functions, impacting everything from headaches and digestion to memory and cognitive functions. In fact, hot flushes can be a symptom of anxiety and heck knows we were all experiencing a ton of that during the pandemic.

Many people were worse off than we were. I have so much admiration for families without the outdoor space or access to laptops that we were fortunate to have. But even though we had all these positives, I knew something had to change. I knew I couldn't afford to spiral downward as I had done in China, and even with my toolkit of habits shaped into a daily routine that had served me so well for so long, I needed to hit the stop button.

At first, of course, I tried to push on through, wearing my badge of busy-ness with pride, but by resisting what was, by resisting reality, I just created more stress, more pain.

And so eventually the realisation that I couldn't do it all, that I couldn't fit the mould of perfectionism I'd crafted for myself, particularly in this crazy new normal, hit me square in the chops. My priorities, what truly matters most in my life, were way out of alignment.

And my mental health was suffering.

So, at the end of 2021, just as I was about to enter my 50th year, I decided to close the doors of my coaching business.

After over six years of working with some incredible clients, it was time to craft a new definition of what success meant for me. It came not long after I took a long sabbatical to press pause, to cut out all the noise and listen to that quiet inner voice in the space in-between, to find some clarity.

And I'm not alone in that need to take time out. Lauren Chiren, CEO and founder of Women of a Certain Stage struggled at work as a result of her symptoms.

"I thought menopause was something that affected 'older' women. I thought it was just hot flushes, mood swings and period stopping. Little did I know!

As a senior leader in financial services, I hit a period of about 18 months of not sleeping well, no more than two hours per night. My confidence and self esteem took a serious knock. Random bouts of palpitations, aching wrists, sore knees and utter loss of self belief led me to leave my job in my early 40's.

Only then, did I embark on a journey of serious self discovery and importantly, awareness of menopause. I discovered, through an amazing family doctor, that going through menopause before 45 is not that uncommon and is called early menopause. As someone who had a child at 37, breast fed for a year and then was on contraception that stopped monthly periods, I never had a bleed after I had my child. In reality, I may have had a premature menopause - menopause that happens under the age of 40. I'll never know.

All I do know, is that 1/100 women go through an early menopause and studies show that somewhere between 1/250 and 1/1000 women experience premature menopause.

This is why raising awareness on all things natural, early premature, surgical and medical menopause is vital at home, work and beyond.

No-one should stumble into their menopausal transition without the knowledge of what it is, the confidence to ask for support and the tools to thrive. That's why I set up womenofacertainstage.com."

The global pandemic shifted a lot of our perspectives on work and life. We experienced loss and pain and gratitude and for some of us, there was the chance to open up to what's truly important for us.

Sometimes when things freeze or stop working, like a computer, for example, you just need to turn it off for a while. I think we're the same; we just find it harder to flick that off switch. When we finally do, the space that's created allows us to do an autopsy of what's been going on inside, investigating what Vishen Lakhiani, founder and CEO of Mindvalley, calls the 'brules' (literally bullsh** rules) we've felt we had to follow, the rut we've settled into and ask ourselves the question 'is this really what I want?' Then, when we switch on again, we see things from a new perspective.

So I left behind the trade-offs I was making, the BS rules I was following, the juggling and the hustling. My priorities had shifted in such a seismic way, none of it mattered anymore. I released some things that I loved to focus on others and took some time to allow whatever was coming next to present itself to me. I spent time with my loved ones and enjoyed that space in-between, where eventually I found the clarity I needed.

Brutal honesty, it took way longer than I hoped! I've never been a patient person, but eventually, I made peace with not doing ALL the things and realigned my life with my priorities - family first, health second, creating a close third. Slowing down, making memories, allowing rather than forcing.

I also acknowledged and accepted that the symptoms which had been escalating steadily over the previous few years were me entering perimenopause.

But it wasn't an easy shift.

Through journaling and my thought awareness practice, I realised that leaving behind the coaching business I'd built from the ground up felt like failing. My identity and self-worth were so tied to my working life that I couldn't see myself as separate from it. And even though that was 100% the right decision, I lost who I actually was for a while.

I also felt that I'd let my clients down, even though they were all incredibly understanding and supportive - I'm so thankful to have worked with such amazing people!

The amount of guilt I'd carried around for not being able to do ALL the things like I used to, mixed uneasily and ironically with the relief I felt after realigning my priorities, so I didn't have to. It's so fascinating to me how we can make a decision in our hearts, yet our thoughts still resist it.

I think as women entrepreneurs we sometimes carry a badge of honour (perhaps only on the inside) for our ability to multitask and play several roles in our work and our life - often at the same time.

When, for whatever reason, we lose that ability or it becomes more challenging, it can hit hard. Competing priorities, lack of quality sleep, energy dips, brain fog, weight gain, hormone shifts, overwhelm - they can all play their part in making us feel less-than.

What I've learned is that when we feel like our best isn't good enough, when we feel like we're losing some imaginary life-race or failing to meet an impossible self-imposed (or culturally positioned) standard, we can remind ourselves we don't need to justify our existence by constantly 'doing' - we really are enough just as we are.

If some balls need to drop along the way, we can let them.

Wherever we are on our journey, we're exactly where we're supposed to be and life's just too short to care what other people (or in my case, my inner perfectionist) might think of that - and frankly, people think a lot less about us than we imagine anyway.

Easy to say, less easy to do, I know.

When I pressed pause, I shared this quote from Rob Bell which summed up so well where I was: "You're leaving one room but you're not yet in the next room, you're crossing the threshold. For a period of time, you're in neither room." In that space of uncertainty, of unknowing, lies vulnerability and doubt.

Enter our supportive habits.

Continuing the computer analogy I mentioned earlier, when we DO switch off for a while, there's a booting-up process when your computer goes through a series of steps to recalibrate, fixing anything that was broken and coming back to equilibrium again.

My Happiness Habits are my boot up programme.

In times of challenge, my habits have always been there to support me. Even as my menopausal symptoms have increased, and my life has changed, my Happiness Habits have remained, albeit with some adaptations. So I wanted to write this new chapter for anyone reading this who might be in the same place, navigating the challenging changes that happen in our bodies and minds as we enter a new life stage, whatever that looks like for you.

First, a bit about what perimenopause is. Dr Shashi Prasad, GP and Menopause specialist:

"Perimenopause, also called Menopause Transition, is the time in a woman's life when the ovaries begin to wind down. On average, it lasts 4–5 years, but it does vary a lot in between women.

Ovaries are the main female reproductive organs, there are two, one lying on either side of the womb or uterus. They have two main functions; producing eggs every month (called ovulation) and producing the main female hormones; oestrogen, progesterone and about 50% of our testosterone, although estrogen is also produced in the adrenal glands and, after menopause, in fat tissues. During perimenopause, the ovaries no longer produce eggs regularly and the amount of hormones produced begin to fluctuate a lot.

As a result our hormonal balance can becomes very chaotic. Periods may begin to get irregular. They can get lighter and more spaced out, or for some women, their periods can become very heavy and painful.

Women may also start to get menopausal symptoms, like brain fog, poor memory and concentration, emotional difficulties and mood problems, hot flushes, and sweats etc. There is a significant fluctuation in the levels of hormones as the ovaries work erratically, so there can be huge ups and downs in symptoms during this phase."

It's important to note also, as Lauren Chiren points out, menopause symptoms may be experienced by women, transgender, non-binary and gender questioning people.

HOW I'VE ADAPTED EACH HABIT

Habit #1 - Thought Awareness

One question I often get asked about this habit is: do I have to meditate to practice thought awareness? My answer is: absolutely not. In fact, as my perimenopause symptoms have progressed, I've found it challenging to maintain my meditation practice some days and I've looked to other ways to notice and analyse my thoughts.

The main one of these is journaling.

Putting pen to paper in a diary or journal is centuries old. And for me it's a habit that dates back to my childhood. We can also combine it with any of the other habits in this book to make them even more powerful.

In fact, I've already touched on it at the end of each chapter, inviting you to make use of a journal to record aspects of the habit I've been discussing. But there's more to journaling than jotting down a few notes, and as many ways to journal as there are people who do it.

Lauren Chiren believes it can be particularly helpful when we're experiencing hormonal changes;

"Whatever stage of life you are at, journaling is profoundly supportive. It helps reflect and builds up a bank of knowledge to help you work out who to approach for support and join the dots on your lifestyle choices and the outcomes they are creating.

With a couple of weeks of building up a journal, a symptoms list, or using an app, you can build a picture of what your hormonal changes are creating for you and therefore a great information guide that you can use to communicate with your doctor or other well-being/health practitioners who can support you on your journey."

I often joke that I came out of the womb holding a notebook and pen. But there's no doubt that a love of scribbling that started young has never left me. From doodling and writing stories as a child, to pouring out my heart in my teenage diary, or documenting life as a new mum on an award-winning blog, I have always had a strange compulsion for writing.

So it was a natural choice to use journaling as part of my cognitive behavioural therapy when I suffered from post-natal depression and the daily act of writing my thoughts and feelings was a practice in looking inwards that was both challenging and a release.

A journal doesn't judge, it merely contains. It holds space for us to explore our inner world, those thoughts and feelings that rise from somewhere deep inside and masquerade as truth.

Whenever I have a challenging series of thoughts or I'm feeling blocked, getting everything out of my head and down on paper is a great way to make sense of what's going on. Often just the act of writing what I'm thinking is enough for me to see that it's just that - thoughts, and that I can take or leave them as I wish. Other times, closing the journal on a piece of internal writing leaves space for my unconscious mind to work on a solution. Often I'll end the writing with a question to help with this.

Lauren Chiren recommends a similar approach if you're if you're journaling your hormonal symptoms;

"Once you have created the physical and psychological space to capture your experiences, reflect on them and consider what messages you're picking up. Then, you can start to consider who may be a good support for you, how you wish to engage them and ask for what you want from them - even if you don't really know what that is!

Some questions to ask yourself are: who should you think about engaging? Family, work colleagues, partners, children, friends, medical/wellbeing/holistic professionals.

How do you prepare? Capture the key messages from your journal, think about who can help you unravel the messages.

What support would you like from your friends, your doctor, your partner, your boss? What information will you share with them? How will you follow up with each other?"

And remember, asking for help is a sign of strength, NOT weakness.

However you practice this habit, through meditating, journaling or just being more aware of that inner voice, remember that our thoughts can have a profound impact on our emotions and results. Be patient with yourself, pause any knee-jerk reactions and know that your thoughts don't have to control or define you.

I also have a free workbook to help you with thought journaling and managing your mindset, using two tools from my former coaching practice - the STEAR Model and Thought Change Ladder. You can download the workbook for free at happinesshabitstransformation.com.

Habit #2 - Inspiration

The feeling of being lost and rudderless when I pressed pause only increased when I closed my business altogether. When I used habit #1 to interrogate my thoughts, I realised one reason for that was that many of my old sources of inspiration didn't fit in with my new life. I knew I needed to discover alternative sources of inspiration as part of my journey into this new season and I set out to do just that, following the three-step process I lay out in chapter five.

I asked myself; who inspires me and how do I want to be inspired now? Then I consciously began unfollowing people on social media that no longer sat comfortably with me and instead followed others, searching for new podcast voices and topics to learn and gain inspiration from and finding books that spoke to my situation and that I could relate to.

If you're feeling like you've lost your purpose, or you're lacking motivation for the things that used to inspire you, it's ok to take a breath and reduce some of that content in your life. The constant barrage of information that hits us every day can be overwhelming at the best of times, so where you can be conscious about what you choose to enter your life.

That might mean unfollowing people on social media that don't resonate with you any longer, and actively finding others who do, or it might mean taking a break altogether - you might discover just what a time sucker it can be!

Habit #3 - Gratitude

As I explained in chapter six, gratitude hasn't always come easily for me and over the past two years that's been true for many of us I'm sure! But while my natural tendency is to come from a place of scarcity, making gratitude a daily habit still allows me to see the sunshine poking through even the cloudiest, rain sodden day - and we certainly get a few of those here in the UK.

This is one habit that I haven't really had to adapt but it's definitely one that continues to serve me in new ways.

As I move into this next stage of my life, I've found I'm comparing myself less with other people, but more with previous versions of myself, noticing that I am stiffer in the morning than I used to be, that I sometimes forget what I'm talking about when I'm chatting with a friend (even before I finish my sentence!), that I'm more tired by the end of the day and that my digestion isn't able to cope with certain foods like it used to.

It's all too easy for negativity to creep in as we age. We forget the bounty of life lessons that our earlier years have taught us and focus on the 'lack' rather than the facts. Even on the toughest days there's so much to be grateful for in my life and my gratitude practice helps me remember that.

Habit #4 - Moving your body

One thing that shocked me the most about entering peri-menopause was learning how the loss of oestrogen could affect my bone health.

Let's talk about bone loss for a sec. Oestrogen, proges-terone and testosterone all have a role in bone health and bone loss can speed up during late perimenopause and continue through post-menopause. If, like me, you're already osteopenic when you enter perimenopause, that bone loss can be even more of a problem.

I was diagnosed with osteopenia in my spine at 45, four years ago. That means my bones are less dense than expected for my age and lifestyle. It also means I'm at a higher risk of fractures and breaks (I've actually broken or fractured bones over six times).

After learning that during perimenopause and menopause our bone density can reduce considerably, I was keen to learn how to increase the strength of my bones and prevent more injuries - for practical reasons as much as anything else - the Mama taxi service can't run without a fully fit driver!

Taking HRT can help to protect against this loss, but the right kinds of exercise can help too.

This is a habit I've definitely had to adapt. I had to leave behind my much loved road running, skiing and any sport or activity (including running around in the garden with my kids) that meant I could fall, and bring in more strength training and walking. I've also had to adapt my diet, increasing the amount of protein I eat to help support the growth of more muscle mass that will support my bones and encourage them to grow stronger.

If you're finding that moving your body in the ways you've always done is less comfortable, you're feeling more aches and pains or you're just not enjoying it as much as you used to, I encourage you to explore other ways of exercising. You 100% do NOT have to join a gym as I've done or start weight lifting (unless you want to!) but strength training of some sort is definitely beneficial in several ways as we age. As Dr Shashi Prasad, notes:

> "Exercises are great for us, but certain types of exercises are especially beneficial for our muscles and bones. Weight-bearing exercises, meaning doing exercises on your feet, with your bones bearing the weight, reduces bone loss after menopause and helps maintain bone mass and bone microarchitecture. Examples include walking, aerobics, running, dancing etc.
>
> Besides this, strength training, which are exercises done against some resistance, is really beneficial in preserving bone and muscle mass and reducing the risk of osteo-sarcopenia. These include, lifting weights, using resistance bands, and push-ups."

You'll find lots of ways to keep moving in my list of 50 ways to move your body in chapter seven. Experiment, find something that fits with your lifestyle so that you can stay consistent and most of all, have fun with it!

Habit #5 - Clarity & dreaming bigger dreams

When I closed my coaching business and began my perimenopause journey, I struggled to create new goals for myself - it's hard to know where you want to get to when you're wading through each day in a funk of brain fog and other symptoms!

But once I'd prioritised self-care and given myself the space and grace to acclimatise to my new normal, I soon realised that without the clarity that goals can bring, I was just drifting and that didn't feel good either.

So I went back to the steps in chapter eight and thought about where I wanted to be, how I wanted to feel, what mattered most to me now. I knew I still wanted to live life with purpose, on purpose, but instead of working forwards towards an ideal life vision, I began by working backwards, deciding what I definitely DID NOT want in my life.

This brought into sharp relief that things I wanted to let go of (like the feelings of guilt I had about closing my business) and allowed space for new things to emerge, like the anticipation of working on the second edition of this book, writing a book with my Mother that documented her own life story and sharing my perimenopause journey hoping it might help others.

Next I thought about my passions - what makes me zing! Writing, painting, connecting, healthy living and exercise, travelling, spending time with my family and friends and so on, and I added those into the mix.

HABITS #6, #7 AND #8

Finally, I worked through exercise #3 from the same chapter and answered the questions to create a picture of what I wanted my life to look like going forward.

Turning that picture into concrete goals felt exciting again, but I was mindful not to fall into the trap of creating an unrealistic plan to meet them. In midlife, many of us have responsibilities for older relatives as well as children, and that 'sandwich' in the middle doesn't have a lot of space for other things! I worked on a realistic plan which extended the deadline for my goals, allowing space for family commitments and my own cup-filling activities like exercise, preparing healthy meals, reading and rest.

I'm a firm believer that we can still have exciting Biscuit Dreams and Smile Goals as we enter new seasons in our lives. The clarity that comes from a designed life allows us to focus in on what matters most and a realistic plan with plenty of time for self-awareness and self-care can protect us from overwhelm.

And yes, I'm still regularly reviewing how I'm shaping up against those goals and plans every week, month and quarter!

Finally, I want to finish with the three habits that I haven't changed since this book was first published: Habits #6

& #7- Smiling and 'but at least' and habit #8 - My daily success party plan. These habits are still a fundamental part of my routine.

In fact, more and more, I'm learning the power that a simple smile can have over my day. During the pandemic, not being able to see people's faces as we talked, not sharing a smile - it was something I missed so much! And when I'm writing or spending time alone, I notice I don't smile as much. So I set myself a reminder because those smile miles are as important as daily steps for a feel good boost.

How about those three little words 'but at least'? Well let me tell you they've been a game changer when my hormones leave me irritable and at the end of my tether. I highly recommend pinning a sticky note to your fridge, mirror, anywhere that you'll see it as a reminder to instantly turn those negatives into positives.

And so we end with the flourish that is celebrating our successes! For a while I did struggle to see the achievements in my day, much the same as I did when I was recovering from postnatal depression. Some days my brain fog, tiredness and lack of motivation meant that I struggled to get much done at all.

But once I began to set myself small milestones again, my end of day party plan kicked back in and now I relish the time I take to look over my goals for the day and celebrate the ones I've nailed. Remember, even the smallest steps forward are progress and that's something to cheer about.

I know how easy it is at this time in our lives to lose ourselves, to feel at the mercy of our hormones, to feel purposeless, unmotivated, frumpy and alone.

If you're coming back to this chapter because it feels more relevant to you now, or if you're reading it as part of your preparation for this time of change in your life, please know that there is a way forward.

Learn as much as you can about perimenopause and menopause - not by Googling, but by seeking out solid, evidence-based advice from respected GPs and specialists like the ones I've listed on my website.

Knowledge is power. Investigate the options that are open to you, decide how you want to feel and how you want to get to that place (whether that's through HRT or other means) and ask for help.

And remember that at a time when so much is in flux, having a solid routine of helpful happiness habits can provide a supportive and grounding base for you to build from.

You'll find a list of perimenopause and menopause resources on my website at happinesshabitstransformation.com

"Someday is not a day of the week"
Denise Brennan Nelson

CHAPTER THIRTEEN

THE END OF OUR JOURNEY TOGETHER... AND THE START OF YOURS

Dear reader,

You now have the eight Happiness Habits, tools and techniques that I used to transform my life, boost my positivity and rediscover a happier, more authentic and truly successful me.

Does this mean I spend my day grinning at rainbows and never feel negative? Honestly, no.

Since I crafted my daily habits into being I've had to deal with some difficult events. I lost my amazing father to heart disease, had another child and collapsed from a massive blood clot requiring a blood transfusion; broke my hand so badly that it's now held together with a metal plate and pins; fractured my elbow playing football in the garden with my kids as I was writing the first draft of this book, got diagnosed with osteopenia (the stage before osteoporosis) and realised I was entering the new journey that is perimenopause.

Challenging things happen. That's just life.

But what my Happiness Habits have gifted me is the positive outlook, perspective, inspiration and motivation to get back in my boots and keep walking. And that's the gift I hope to have passed on to you in these pages.

I wholeheartedly believe it's ok to feel like there's something missing from your life. Please forgive yourself for feeling resentful, lost or somehow 'less than' and take the time to design how you want to feel instead. Release yourself from any feelings of guilt and create your life courageously, with exciting dreams, achievable plans and consistent action. Commit to defining success on YOUR terms and celebrate even the smallest victories along your journey with gusto!

We've come to the end of our journey together. I hope that you've enjoyed reading this book and perhaps taken some inspiration from my story. Most of all I hope you've found it useful in helping you to begin crafting a routine with time to focus on YOU, releasing you from the habit of negativity, boosting your self-esteem and helping you to dream and plan out YOUR ideal life.

I know from personal experience that the first few weeks after reading a book or taking a course can make or break whether the lessons you've learned become a transformative part of your life. So indulge me when I say this, please put what you've learned from our time together into practice. Take action in any way that's meaningful for you, but take action. Because even though we're at the end of our journey together, your Happiness Habits Transformation is just about to begin.

I'm so excited for you!

michelle

READER-EXCLUSIVE RESOURCES

Unlock exclusive resources to help you in your own
Happiness Habits Transformation at

happinesshabitstransformation.com

ACKNOWLEDGEMENTS

I loved the whole process of writing this book but bringing our thoughts and ideas to life on paper is one of the most challenging things that anyone can do, and there are people I must thank for their help along the way.

To Stewart, my husband and soul mate, for your patience, for always believing in me and keeping me grounded and balanced. I love you so much.

To my incredible children, Amelia and Sebastian, who remind me each and every day that everything happens for a reason and they are that reason over and over again. (And for being brilliant when I fractured my elbow during the final draft of the first edition and needed you to be extra helpful!)

To my amazing Mother for showing me that courage and determination, personal choice, growth and love can triumph over any circumstance in our lives. You are my inspiration.

To the rest of my family for supporting me and checking in from time to time to see how I was getting on, but never pressuring me as much as I was pressuring myself.

To everyone who provided comments and shared their stories for the book; Zaz, Vic, George, Lucy, Nila, Julie, Vicki, Cheryl, Juliet and Carol Ann you are all amazing.. Special thanks also to Juliet for being my health consultant for chapter seven - I'm so grateful for your advice - and to Ceri Gillett for being there when I wobbled during the first edition.

To Lauren Chiren and Dr Shashi, who provided valuable insights and comments in the creation of the new chapter about my menopause journey, for the 2nd edition.

To Alex Hardy and Shireen Peermohamed at Harbottle & Lewis, and Jane Graham Maw at Graham Maw Christie for their helpful guidance and advice and to Stu Adams, my brother in law, for being utterly amazing in bringing us all together (and just brilliant in general).

To the Shanghai Mamas who came into my life when I truly needed them - Amy, Holly, Mimi, Kathy, Corinne, Maggie, Hilda, Karen, Tonya, Carol, Rhian, Christina, Cath, Alyssa, Liz, Sirimon, Lou, Miyhun and Clara. And a special mention to Barbara - you touched so many lives including mine, you taught me to love life and live it to the full. Shine bright beautiful - we love you and miss you so much.

To James Shaw and Anthony Barlow at Matthew James Publishing for their patience, believing in this idea from the beginning, supporting a second bite of the cherry and for helping me navigate through the world of publishing.

To my incredible coaching clients who welcomed me into their world and travelled on a journey of self-discovery with me with openness, dedication and courage. I learned so much from you.

Thank you and much love to you all x

NOTES

1   Hebbar, Shripad et al. "Reference Ranges of Amniotic Fluid Index in Late Third Trimester of Pregnancy: What Should the Optimal Interval between Two Ultrasound Examinations Be?" Journal of Pregnancy 2015 (2015): 319204. PMC. Web. 23 May 2018

2   Have No Fear, the Brain is Here! How Your Brain Responds to Stress https://kids.frontiersin.org/article/10.3389/frym.2017.00071

3   Confirmation Bias - https://www.sciencedaily.com/terms/confirmation_bias.htm

4   The Science Behind Meditation, Dr David Cox, Dr Amishi Jha, Andy Puddicombe, Headspace, 2013.

5   How many neurons make a human brain?, The Guardian, Feb 2012; https://www.theguardian.com/science/blog/2012/feb/28/how-many-neurons-human-brain (accessed Jan 2018)

6   If you'd like to use a meditation app to help you start or restart your meditation practice I thoroughly recommend the Headspace or Calm apps

7   A Theory of Human Motivation, A. H. Maslow (1943), Originally Published in Psychological Review, 50, 370-396.

8 "Who inspires Tony Robbins", interview by Marie Speed in Success Magazine, Nov 17, 2016. https://www.success.com/article/who-inspires-tony-robbins

9 "What I Know For Sure," Oprah Winfrey, 2014, Pan Macmillan,. p110.

10 Counting Blessings Versus Burdens: An Experimental Investigation of Gratitude and Subjective Well-Being in Daily Life, Robert A. Emmons, Michael E. McCullough, Journal of Personality and Social Psychology, 2003, Vol. 84, No. 2, 377–389.

11 "The Gifts of Imperfection", Brené Brown, 2010, Hazelden Publishing, p77-78.

12 Counting blessings in early adolescents: an experimental study of gratitude and subjective well-being, Froh JJ, Sefick WJ, Emmons RA., Journal of School Psychology 46 (2008) 213–233.

13 "Gratitude as a Psychotherapeutic Intervention," by Robert A Emmons, Ph.D. Dept. of Psychology, University of California, Davis and Robin S. Stern, Associate Director of the Yale Center for Emotional Intelligence, Journal of Clinical Psychology Volume 69, Issue 8, pages 846–855, August 2013.

14 Recommended levels of physical activity for adults aged 18 - 64 years; World Health Organisation Global Strategy on Diet, Physical Activity and Health; http://www.who.int/dietphysicalactivity/factsheet_adults/en/ (accessed 22/1/18)

15 Mood Enhancement Persists for up to 12 Hours following Aerobic Exercise: A Pilot Study, Jeremy S. Sibold & Kathleen M. Berg, Perceptual & Motor Skills; Oct 2010, Vol. 111 Issue 2, p333-342

16   A Randomized Controlled Trial of the Effect of Aerobic Exercise Training on Feelings of Energy and Fatigue in Sedentary Young Adults with Persistent Fatigue; Puetz T, W, Flowers S, S, O'Connor P, J; Psychother Psychosom 2008;77:167-174

17   Quoted in "100 Simple Secrets of the Best Half of Life", David Niven PhD, HarperCollins, 2005: "People who could identify a goal they were pursuing were 19 percent more likely to feel satisfied with their lives and 26 percent more likely to feel positive about themselves." – Krueger 1998

18   Paul Ekman, PhD., "Universal Facial Expressions of Emotion", California Mental Health Research Digest, Vol. 8, Autumn 1970, No 4.

19   Research conducted by OnePoll for shoe brand Moshulu and supported by Dr. Jessamy Hubbard: https://www.moshulu.co.uk/the-smile-scale/ (accessed Jan 2018)

20   "Smile Intensity in Photographs Predicts Longevity", Ernest L. Abel, Michael L. Kruger, Psychological Science, Vol 21, Issue 4, pp. 542 - 544, First Published February 26, 2010

21   Charles Darwin, "The Expression of emotion in man and animals", 1896.

22   Tara Kraft and Sarah Pressman, "Grin and bear it, The Influence of Manipulated Facial Expression on the Stress Response", 24 Sept 2012, Psychological Science, Vol 23, Issue 11, pp. 1372-1378

23   "Anticipatory and post hoc cushioning strategies: Optimism and defensive pessimism in "risky" situations", Norem, J.K. & Cantor, N. Cogn Ther Res (1986) 10: 347.

24   Ron Gutman, "The Hidden Power Of Smiling", March 2011, TED2011, at www.TED.com

25   Teresa Amabile & Steven J Kramer, "The Power of Small Wins," Harvard Business Review, May 2011.

26   "Explainer: What is dopamine?" Science for students website https://www.sciencenewsforstudents.org/article/explainer-what-dopamine

27   "Habits - A Repeat Performance", David T Neal, Wendy Wood, and Jeffrey M Quinn, Current Directions in Psychological Science 15, No 4 (2006)

28   The Editors of Encyclopaedia Britannica, Habit, Encyclopaedia Britannica,Inc., Sept 08, 2014, https://www.britannica.com/topic/habit-behaviour, access date Jan 10, 2018

29   Graybiel, A.M. (1998). The basal ganglia and chunking of action repertoires. Neurobiology of learning and memory, 70 119-36

30   Duhigg, C. (2012). The power of habit: Why we do what we do in life and business. New York: Random House

31   The "Four Stages for Learning Any New Skill" learning stages model was developed at Gordon Training International by its employee Noel Burch; http://www.gordontraining.com/free-workplace-articles/learning-a-new-skill-is-easier-said-than-done/

32   In a study, researchers found that tooth flossing was more likely to stay as a habit if people embedded it within an existing habit that was already part of their routine https://www.psychologytoday.com/blog/dont-delay/201310/you-can-develop-desired-health-behaviors

33   How are habits formed: Modelling habit formation in the real world, Lally, P., van Jaarsveld, C. H. M., Potts, H. W. W. and Wardle, J. (2010), Eur. J. Soc. Psychol., 40: 998–1009. doi: 10.1002/ejsp.67

Quote by Jim Rohn, America's Foremost Business Philosopher, reprinted with permission from SUCCESS ©2016. For more information on Jim and his popular personal achievement resources visit www.JimRohn.com

All website links were accessed
Dec 2017 - February 2018
unless otherwise stated.